MW01143994

**Published by Morning Dove Press**
Eastern Canada's Christian Publishing House
Nova Scotia, Canada

**His Sweet Sustenance**

Cover Art by Doretta Zinck
Edited by Morning Dove Press
Designed by Holymakerel Creative

A Morning Dove Press book
Paperback ISBN 978-1-998057-02-3
E-Book ISBN 978-1-998057-03-0

Published and printed in Canada.
www.morningdovepress.ca

# His Sweet Sustenance

## Reflecting On My Father's Provision & Pursuit

Donna,
Thank you for
all your love and
support! Love you
so much! ♡ Julianna
Davidson

By Julianna Davidson

Surely your goodness and love will follow me all the days of my life, and I will dwell in the house of the LORD forever.

— Psalm 23:6

# Dedication

To my beautiful friends and family whose stories have been interwoven with mine and shared throughout this book. I am blessed to walk through the trials and triumphs of life with you. Our sweet Saviour has used your spirit-led hearts to minister to mine in the most memorable ways.

I love you deeply and will always be thankful for you.

# Table of Contents

Prologue     1

Introduction: The Source of My Sustenance     7

Understanding Spiritual Sustenance     18

Exchanging Fear for Sustaining Faith     30

Exchanging Brokenness for Sustaining Hope     40

Exchanging Longings for Sustaining Contentment     50

Exchanging Loneliness for Sustaining Security     66

Exchanging Striving for a Sustaining Perspective     84

Exchanging Grumbling for Sustaining Gratitude     92

Exchanging Sorrow For Sustaining Joy     104

Exchanging Insufficiency for Sustaining Abundance     114

Exchanging Anger for Sustaining Grace to Forgive     126

An Invitation to Embracing Sustaining Peace     146

The Abundance of His Sustenance     152

Epilogue     168

# Prologue

Very early in the writing of this book, God gave me this vision of a bird; a tiny, vulnerable bird who was at the mercy of the wind and the rain. However, within the elements, it remained calm as it found nourishment in the palm of its Maker's hand. The nourishment was readily available for this tiny creature, it just had to seek it out. In my imagination, this bird was at rest, finding nourishment in a safe haven, flowing abundantly with birdseed. It was still, peaceful, satisfied, and sustained; entirely purposed for the bird's ability to thrive and survive.

When I think of a beautiful, little bird fluttering its wings, I am reminded of how fragile it is. In comparison to other creatures, it is relatively small and common; birds are everywhere! They could easily be overlooked, not because they are less majestic and beautiful but because they seem to be a dime a dozen. Unlike more exotic animals, such as lions, zebras, or certain insects- birds are everywhere around the world. Consequently, one could say they seem less magnificent in that sense. I in no way agree with this; they are amazing and I remain jealous that I cannot fly.

There are so many Bible verses that remind us that even the birds are important to God. He cares for them and sustains them through the earthly seasons. Be encouraged by all these reminders of God's everpresent care for His creatures. If this common creature is on His mind, even more so, we are in His heart. He will sustain us through the seasons of our lives; those who He cherishes and have chosen, made in His very image.

Luke 12:24 says, *"Consider the ravens: They do not sow or reap, they have no storeroom or barn; yet God feeds them. And how much more valuable you are than birds!"* Amen to that! Matthew 10:29 shows us the attention of the Father, saying, *"Are not two sparrows sold for a penny? Yet not one of them will fall to the ground outside your Father's care."* Then in Matthew 26:9, this concept is reiterated again, comparing our worth to the birds, by saying, *"Look at the birds of the air; they do not sow or reap or store away in barns, and yet your heavenly Father feeds them. Are you not much more valuable than they?"*

In Psalms, the author writes that even the birds make their dwelling in the place of God.

*How lovely is your dwelling place, LORD Almighty!*

*My soul yearns, even faints, for the courts of the LORD; my heart and my flesh cry out for the living God.*

*Even the sparrow has found a home, and the swallow a nest for herself, where she may have her young— a place near your altar, LORD Almighty, my King and my God.*

*- Psalms 84:1-3*

This entire stanza just rings with a sense of peace and glory. A place where a mother chooses to have her young! A place our souls yearn to be! Our dwelling place should be in His presence. We do not have heaven yet, and boy am I excited for it, but we do have the hope of heaven through the Holy Spirit who can abide within us.

I want to rest near His altar. In Psalm 91:4, it declares that *"He will cover you with His feathers, and under His wings you will find refuge."* Look at that- He joined the metaphor too! I just love that! When the harsh winters come and the wind blows and creates a disruption to my comfort and survival, I want to rest and find solace under His wing. I want the protection of His feathers over my little, frail, and fragile body and soul.

About eight years ago, I was doing a Bible study with friends on the book of Ruth. If you aren't familiar with the book, it's about a woman whose husband died, and instead of reuniting with her family, she decided to honour her mother-in-law, who also had lost her husband, and remained with her. Ruth was intentional in following her mother-in-law, even so much as to move with her to a place where she would be ostracized for her cultural background. Her choice to follow her mother-in-law, Naomi, certainly wasn't the easiest option available to her, but her actions showed character, loyalty, and captivating faith in the Lord. Ruth and Naomi were humbled by their circumstances of death and famine but they continued to listen to the Lord's leading. In doing so, the Lord used a man named Boaz, who was of reputable social standing, and who became enchanted by Ruth's presence working in his fields, and extended kindness to her and provided for her and Naomi's needs. There are so many more details that make the story so enthralling. Ruth and Boaz end up falling in love and have what I would call quite the proposal story. God uses their faithfulness and loyalty to bless each other and redeem their circumstances. It's such a beautiful reflection of God's redemption in our lives.

As I studied Ruth, I was just coming out of an extremely heavy and dark season in my life where I was completely broken. I had made terrible decisions in my desire to be pursued that did not honour God (that's an entirely separate book for when God gives me the grace and vision for it). It brought turmoil and heartache to myself and others. It was a dark time. A time when I had failed and felt completely useless and shameful; utterly broken. In comparison to Ruth, I felt the complete opposite in how I had handled myself. I was healing, but the wounds were still somewhat fresh and the scars seemed so entrenched in my soul that I could barely see hope.

Although I was attending this Bible study, I can't say I was on a spiritual high. Most of the concepts that we focused on in the book I could see were places where my character and integrity had failed. It was humbling but the Lord was gracious and gentle throughout the study. He used it to minister to my heart and reveal what redemption could look like. We finished the bible study and our leaders asked us to write down a message that the Lord laid on our hearts upon the completion of the bible study. What I wrote hangs on my hope board all these years later and I can say, it has come to fulfillment.

Just as God redeemed Naomi and Ruth's circumstances, He will redeem, sustain and restore your circumstances. He will not rest, but be relentless in His pursuit of you and the redemption of your life. For He is your Redeemer!

My hope board is something I have developed over the last decade that is filled with verses, quotes, song lyrics, and a few prophetic notes of encouragement that I appreciate, and can depend on, to refuel my tank when I need it. I wrote this eight years ago when it was an act of faith to believe it could come true. I would say that even then, I was skeptical because I was still so broken. I wrote this in my darkest season, not knowing how this promise would play out. Looking back, I find the order of these three verbs so amazing; redeem, sustain, and restore. About two years later, God gave me the words Redeem & Redemption as the overarching theme for that season in my life. He told me to look with anticipation for how He was going to redeem my life. I needed to be pursuing Him to see how He was doing this. He overwhelmed me and blessed me in a season of redemption. He redeemed my heart, friendships, and how I viewed myself and my worth. While there are still remnants of the scars, they do not go as deep and He continues to heal me even today from memories that can be hard to forget. He is so gracious. I truly feel like some of my scars and baggage don't even belong to my story anymore; it feels like a different life and person. I have seen His redemption.

This brings us to now; for about a year, God has laid the words Sustain & Sustenance on my mind and heart. He has requested the same task for me; to be looking for how He will sustain me, in many different avenues of life. He has encouraged me to be looking for it with hope and expectation.

When I wrote this proclamation over my life, I didn't even know the meaning behind the words He gave me. I wrote He will redeem, sustain and restore your circumstances. It took me eight years to realize; I wrote them down in the same order that He has been giving them to me to focus on over the years. Redeem first and now sustain. So I am wondering if restoration comes next? It makes me wonder if it wasn't a proclamation, but more of a prophecy that I didn't have a sweet clue about at the time. I love how God's ability to work and move has nothing to do with our personal state and understanding. I am so thankful for that! I await eagerly my season of restoration, but for now, I set my sights on His sustainment of me.

I invite you to join me as I reminisce and reflect on God's pursuit and provision over my life. He continues to sustain me. I mean on an eternal level; my soul. My physical body will still eventually meet destruction. Once I hit thirty, I have been seeing the slow decay. Just kidding....kind of....But take heart, He is the lover of your soul. That is where His concern lies. This perspective brings me confident peace. My prayer is that it gives you the same hope.

# Introduction: The Source of My Sustenance

*Even to your old age and gray hairs I am He, I am
He who will sustain you. I have made you and I will carry you;
I will sustain you and I will rescue you.*

*- Isaiah 46:4*

It was a gorgeous summer day in early July, as the afternoon sun shimmered against the waves. I was officially on summer break. Being back home in Nova Scotia at my parent's home on the lake was making it feel like I was finally on vacation. The refreshing water was inviting. It was effortless to relax while looking out at this beautiful view each day. The humid air made the breeze coming off the water increasingly appealing.

It was the perfect day for a paddleboard. Paddleboarding has become a revitalizing habit in my life, where I put on a peaceful playlist, bring my trusty, labrador-retriever pup, and hit the lake for some reflection and enjoyment. It quiets my heart and centers me, often becoming a time of prayer and worship as I listen to songs that draw me closer to Jesus. That day, my excitement and motivation enticed me to paddle down to the other end of the lake. Although it wasn't a huge lake, it still was a reasonable distance that I had never ventured before. It would take roughly over an hour, but I knew I could foresee the sweet reward of leisurely laying out on my board, enjoying the wind, trusting it would carry me back to our end of the lake: home.

I slapped on some sunscreen and off we went. It was one of those moments where I was truly thankful for my current reality and wanted to let those positive thoughts intentionally dwell in the forefront of my mind during this afternoon trip. My frisky pup, Harley, sat up front as her tongue dangled out of her mouth and her head turned from side to side, taking in the summer sights. Her tail wagged back and forth slowly, mopping up water from each side of the board as her tail skimmed the surface of the water. She looked prideful as she surveyed her kingdom of wind and waves. It was an endearing sight and there is something that thrills my soul about seeing my furry companion enjoy the activity as much as I do.

I smiled as I worked to break through the waves with my paddle. It was challenging but enjoyable; a task I felt I could manage well. My mind kept anticipating how relaxing the ride back would be as the wind would be working with me and not against me upon my return... Put in the hard work first, then sit back and enjoy! This was my vision and mantra.

Over an hour later, I had set my sights on my personal goal and destination that signaled to turn back for home; a small island that I would curve around. The wind had gained more strength at this end of the lake and created the need for more forceful strokes in the water. As I dug into my depleted resources of strength, I made the last strides with the paddle and rounded the other side of the island, adjusting the direction of my paddleboard back toward my final destination. I accomplished my goal, and now I would reap the benefits of my hard work. I did realize that the force of the wind would carry me quickly and I would want to be aware of my path- so it might require sitting with the paddle and making slight adjustments with my oar to stay on course.

I had originally imagined laying out, soaking up the quiet tranquility with my eyes closed, unconcerned with where I would drift as it would gently and eventually lead me home. Although this reality wasn't quite unfolding as I had imagined, it could still work! I could be flexible and still enjoy the ride back. I sat down and felt a twinge of anxiety as I regretted my choice of bringing my one oar and not the other attachment to make it a kayaking paddle. It would have been much more efficient and helpful, but I hadn't anticipated the wind's strength or sudden change of direction. When I left the house, everything looked manageable.

I fought the racing current and quickly understood this wasn't going to be what I had envisioned at all. If I didn't stand up and actively paddle against the current with my residual strength, the wind would carry me rapidly across the lake to the other side, even farther from home. My dog, who had been relaxing at the front of the paddleboard, was now feeling uneasy, standing up, whimpering, and looking for a quick exit to safety, which was too far away at this point. I tried to calm her and got her to sit back down, but it was clear her rest had also come to a swift end.

I was disheartened as I sat there, knowing that the longer I waited before fighting back and taking action against this raging wind, the harder my journey home would be. I stood up with disappointment and began to paddle. It was much more difficult at this point in the trip than ever before; even more so because I had used up most of my energy for the initial part of the journey. I felt like I didn't have much endurance left in me, certainly not enough to make it home. I was irritated by the lack of control I had in my current situation and the fact that out on this lake my power was seemingly pathetic in comparison to the waves. This was not at all what I had dreamed of as my rewarding trip back home. It was increasingly difficult and unyielding to my fatigue; a challenge I saw as unmanageable.

I focused, one stroke at a time, avoiding looking up as often as possible to refrain from being overwhelmed by the tumultuous journey ahead. I started praying for strength and just talking to God like He was by my side with a paddle in hand, also fighting these waves with me; like two friends. I muttered a few complaints about how this wasn't what I wanted but we'd get through it. I tried not to entertain fearful thoughts of being overtaken by the waves, resigning myself to the knowledge that it would be fine, but simply embarrassing if I ended up stranded on the other side of the lake. My family would eventually come to find me. Then, I laughed a little bit, knowing that if this was my worst problem, it was going to be just fine. I was trying to keep perspective amidst the chaos. In the thick of my struggle, I audibly asked God what I often do... "Okay God, what will this be a metaphor for? How can this situation apply to life? How will you use this to teach me something?" It seemed to me, this was His call to me: His whisper in the wind.

In the last decade, God has often used metaphors to teach me various truths. I don't know if it's just something that my brain does to process things or if it's a way he chooses to speak to me. Regardless of its reason, it has become a way for me to think and grow in my spiritual life. He often uses metaphors to show me something in a new way or reveal more understanding of His grace and love. Even more often, these lessons encourage the growing and molding of myself in my relationship with Christ. So I asked Him these questions with confidence, knowing I didn't need the answer immediately...what I currently needed was to get back home... I knew the answer would be revealed later, in His time, when my mind and heart could absorb it.

When I finally arrived back home, I was utterly exhausted. I had used all of my strength to return and dug deeper physically than I knew I could. If someone could have foretold me how this afternoon would have realistically unfolded, I would have definitely refused and opted for a different, more comfortable plan.

I realized once my feet were placed firmly on shore, I had been holding a lot of tension in my body. I looked back down the lake from where I had just come and thanked God for giving me the continued strength to get home. I had planned to stay close to the shore and so I had not brought a life jacket with me. The wind had pushed me far from the shore, into the center of the lake. I thanked God, as I knew that it could have been a much worse situation had we tipped in the center of the lake or been blown to the other side. I pledged to bring a life jacket with me next time, acknowledging that plans don't often unfold as we envision. It would be good to be prepared when things go sideways.

As the days passed, my thoughts carried me back to my little voyage down the lake. I prayed for spiritual application and a metaphor started to emerge. My adventure down the lake is a lot like the journey we experience in life. We have plans and personal dreams, envisioning how things are going to play out. We do our best to control things in order to ensure they will be the way we imagined, all the while anticipating how wonderful it will feel and the various longings that will be met inside of us when it comes to fruition. What are some of those dreams for you? That job or promotion? A beautiful and long-lasting marriage? Being able to give birth and raise healthy children? That highly desirable home, automobile, or vacation? The blessing of a healthy body for you and your loved ones? A dependable friend who is there through thick and thin? What realities would fulfill the longings in your heart?

Proverbs 13:12 tells us that *"hope deferred makes the heart sick, but a longing fulfilled is a tree of life."* I have seen both sides of this proverb in my life and it rings true. The dreams we carry are often beautiful and healthy. However, life in this broken world has a way of shattering some of those intentions. You get to the place you have been preparing for and it all unfolds very differently than you expected. Sickness, rejection, death, divorce, betrayal, or a loss of any kind are just a few examples of hopes being deferred or sometimes, completely obliterated.

In many situations, you have very little choice or control but you must take some sort of action in order to survive. The only control you have is how you will respond to your disappointing, or even devastating, circumstances. When you are in that moment of realization, how do you choose to respond? With disenchantment or hopelessness? With anger or rage? Do you give-up? Do you fight back? Do you desperately try to change the outcome for yourself? Maybe you've tried all of these reactions in those moments when the hopelessness of life creeps in. I know I have... All we know is that we have to get through it. In some circumstances, we don't even know how or where to begin with our response.

What I want to tell you is this: in those critical junctures, when you don't feel like you have enough strength to even counter back, you are not required to do it in your own strength. You can rely on God's strength and sustainment. He tells us in the book of Matthew, *"Come to me, all you who are weary and burdened, and I will give you rest (Matthew 11:28-30)."* Isn't that a wonderful promise? He's calling you to Him, all the time, but makes a point here to acknowledge especially those times when life is hard and makes your heart feel heavy.

> *He's calling you to Him, all the time, but makes a point here to acknowledge especially those times when life is hard and makes your heart feel heavy.*

In Isaiah, He reminded the Israelites of this promise, "*Even to your old age and gray hairs I am He, I am He who will sustain you. I have made you and I will carry you; I will sustain you and I will rescue you*" (Isaiah 46:4). Since God is a God who never changes, we have this same promise to cling to now as well. This hope was the beginning of a new realization for me; a declaration that has brought freedom and security.

Sustenance refers to the maintenance of someone or something in order to survive. As basic as that sounds, sometimes that's just what we need! Depending on your circumstances, maybe all you can see is a need for survival and a way to get through the pain of that particular trial. If that's what you need, take it! However, I want to encourage you that in all of life's circumstances, you can have confidence in the wonderful expectation that the outcome of His sustenance is the promise of His blessings over you. His plans are better and His ways are higher. He has good plans for your life!

What God has been gently teaching me is that He is the one who sustains me. His character is the source of my sustenance. His power provides the sustainment I need within my circumstances and will continue to do so. He has been faithful to me before and will remain faithful in the future as well. Trust me, this has been a lesson that I am still learning and has been thirty-four years in the making.

While I acknowledge this as truth, I still have questions about why He has allowed some things to happen in my life or worry about what the future will look like. I still fall into the trap of being fearful for the future or resentful about the past, creating a dark spiral of thoughts in my mind. Possibly a similar place to where you have also found yourself. However, as He teaches me about His sustaining power, I am learning to leave the spiral and get back sooner to a place of rest and a calming trust in His sustenance over my life. I am no expert, but merely an observer of His gentle leading and hopeful truth. I hope to encourage you with the encounters that I have seen in my life of His rescue and supply. He has sustained me through so many seasons and circumstances.

My prayer is that as you read through this book, you will be encouraged by what my experiences have taught me while also being able to sift through your own journey to see where Christ has sustained you. If you feel like you can't see His sustainment in your story, I pray that your heart and mind would be revealed to His care and love for you. If you are His child, I promise you it is there! While this truth requires letting go of control, an effective way to build faith is to look back at your life to see where He has proven to be faithful before. This gives you hope for the future, and hope, my friend, is a wonderful thing.

As we slog through the realization that life isn't unfolding the way we imagined, I dare you to entertain the idea that it could be unfolding in an even better way than you could have ever planned or designed. You just have to be willing to let go of your timeline and control and to seek His will and His way. Come join me for this life-altering adventure!

His character is the
source of my sustenance.

# Understanding Spiritual Sustenance

*Remain in me, as I also remain in you. No branch can bear fruit by itself; it must remain in the vine. Neither can you bear fruit unless you remain in Me.*
*— John 15:4*

Several years ago, God spoke to me through a verse in Jeremiah. To me, it is the perfect picture of what I view as spiritual sustenance.

*But blessed is the one who trusts in the LORD, whose confidence is in Him. They will be like a tree planted by the water that sends out its roots by the stream. It does not fear when heat comes; its leaves are always green. It has no worries in a year of drought and never fails to bear fruit.*
*— Jeremiah 17:7-8*

These verses describe many things that I hope to embody in my day-to-day life; not just in the moments where I have an epiphany of God's love and grace, but in the regular, routine moments. It talks about the abundance that the tree has in the drought; always green, continuing to bear fruit. I want to be like that tree: a visual representation of a spiritual transformation within my soul, that others can be encouraged through. I printed this verse off and framed it in my living room as a reminder of how I want to walk through this life. I want to not only have my life maintained by God's presence and leading, but to live with abundant hope, joy, and the spiritual fruit to encourage others. I hope this verse and concept can be an encouragement to you as well.

It is important when discussing spiritual sustenance that we pause to define what it actually means. For years, I have had the phrase unbroken connection floating around in my mind when I think about what I want my relationship with Jesus to be like. My ambition is to walk daily with Jesus, in a state of unbroken connection where He is a part of my thoughts, conversations, and reactions throughout the day; not out of legalism but out of an intimate relationship. I want it to be a natural state rather than something I strive to do. As Jesus said in John 15:4, *"Remain in me, as I also remain in you. No branch can bear fruit by itself; it must remain in the vine. Neither can you bear fruit unless you remain in me."*

> *My ambition is to walk daily with Jesus, in a state of unbroken connection where He is a part of my thoughts, conversations, and reactions throughout the day; not out of legalism but out of an intimate relationship.*

As we delve into this, I want to emphasize the idea of grace in spiritual sustenance and how God fulfills our needs as we remain in Him. To remain in Him is to be in sync with the Holy Spirit. In this sense, we are relying on our communion with the Holy Spirit, living within us, to overflow into our actions, which in turn affects the way we think and perceive others in our daily interactions. For this to be accomplished, it requires us to live intentionally- seeking after oneness with Jesus, and to be in constant conversation with our Father through prayer in the midst of our circumstances. To remain in Him means to understand that He is our source for sustenance; not our own strength or our own will, but continually recognizing that He is where we need to run to be filled.

His Grace plays into this because our Father is full of mercy when we are distracted or lose perspective and step out of sync with Him. In my personal walk, I frequently come back to Him, knowing that I have not held a kingdom perspective but a very self-absorbed perception of my circumstances. I never feel rebuked in these moments. What I do sense is the attitude of a father who would be filled with love and joy upon their prodigal daughter's return. We pick up where we left off and I can immediately sense His presence in my perceptions and attitudes toward my current circumstances. However often this realignment needs to happen, I am always reassured by His presence that abiding in Him is how I thrive.

When we walk with Jesus and look to Him to maintain our hearts and minds, we can focus on Him and have a kingdom perspective rather than an earthly one. What I mean by this is to focus on the things that are important in light of eternity rather than the momentary distractions that seem so important, but are relatively inconsequential on an eternal level. Certain circumstances might seem important in the current moment, but will they hold meaning in a day or a week? When we walk with this conviction, we will likely respond differently to people and situations because we are functioning with a mindset that is prudent and wise rather than impulsive and self-serving.

When I choose to function this way, I am able to walk with an eternal perspective; responding to events, people, and hardships with much more grace than I ever could in my own strength. Consequently, it's also not difficult to tell when I am out of sync with the Holy Spirit, as I can see my impatience, selfishness, and pride quickly surface in how I deal with the people in my life.

Tying it back to the verse from Jeremiah 17, the tree rooted by the stream is able to bear fruit regardless of the circumstances because the fruit is not dependent on what is happening in life but on Who is providing for it.

Trusting in the Lord can be so difficult. I find that my heart and mind are so fickle. As a result, I find I have more frequent breaks in my connection with Jesus than the constant peace that He can supply for me. I am often disappointed or even embarrassed at my reactions or responses throughout the day. These blush-worthy moments seem to occur more often when I am out of step with my Saviour; when I haven't spent time with Him for days and am not walking in any sense of continued connection. I am learning that, when we become consumed by this earthly turmoil and fight against the flesh, it can gnaw

> *We will experience seasons of suffering– that earthly ache– but we always have Him as our source of strength and deliverance in the middle of those battles.*

away at the trust we have and the opportunity to be held in our heavenly Father's sustaining sovereignty over our lives. We will experience seasons of suffering- that earthly ache- but we always have Him as our source of strength and deliverance in the middle of those battles.

David encourages us in Psalm 23:5, when he declares in thanksgiving to the Lord, *"You prepare a table before me in the presence of my enemies."* This verse alludes to the fact that God will meet us in the midst of our trials and provide nourishment to our weary souls. Notice though, that he says, in the presence of my enemies. We can infer from this that God is not removing him from the trial, but meeting him within it. What peace to know that we are not alone in the midst of life's storms. One of the greatest temptations we face is choosing how we think and respond in those moments when we are discouraged. We can be drawn closer to the Holy Spirit, or we can pull away from our source of strength, and see the consequences of that choice in our relationship with God and our interactions with others.

So what happens to our hearts and minds that these daily, mundane incidents can bring out such faithless responses? Even when we are walking in faith and doing our best to love others the way Jesus exemplified, the world creeps in with its lies and "truths" that pull us away from our loving Father.

Growing up in Nova Scotia, a rock chip in one's windshield was not something that happened too often but when it did occur, people got them fixed right away. In my twenty-three years of living in Nova Scotia, I remember two incidents of our family getting rock chips in our windows. It always required hastily booking an appointment to fix it before the crack spread further throughout the windshield and ruined its integrity. If you could catch it soon enough, the damage could be less extensive. Tending to this matter quickly ensured that your windshield could continue carrying out its purpose of protected vision while driving.

When I was twenty-three years old, I moved out west where things were a whole lot different. Half-ton pickups, large SUVs, and an overwhelming amount of transport trucks dominate the streets. It's the wild wild west and things are flying everywhere- including rocks! In the ten years I've lived in Northern Alberta, I've gotten more rock chips, cracks, and ruined windshields than I can count on both of my hands! It's not uncommon to see vehicles driving around with huge cracks in their windshield, spreading from side to side. To make matters worse, our roads have giant potholes that help a chip to give birth to a taunting crack that spins and curls through the glass, eventually destroying the entire windshield.

Coming from my "out East" experience, I was shocked by this. At first, I tried my best to get to the professionals quickly, but I usually didn't make it there in time to save the windshield. My colleagues used to laugh at me in my first few years when I immediately went and got my windshield fixed or replaced. After the fifth windshield replacement, I was fed up paying for windshields and decided I was going to let the crack remain. However, it had crossed my windshield right across my line of vision. Sometimes, when the sun hit the crack, it would make it incredibly difficult to see as the rays of light were almost multiplied by beaming through the fractured glass. So whether safe or not, I had decided to rebel against my Nova Scotian roots and let it remain. I was now a seasoned veteran of Grande Prairie roads and the calloused toll it took on my trusty automobile.

One October when my parents came out to visit, my dad was horrified to know I was driving around with this huge crack, which he stated was compromising our sight and safety. We were going on a bit of a road trip, so upon his request, I got the windshield replaced. Within a week of getting this windshield replaced, another rock hit the windshield about ½ inch away from the very edge. It was so close to the edge that I couldn't see it from inside the car. I didn't notice when it initially happened and when I did notice, it was because it had already started creeping across the windshield and into my line of sight. I was so annoyed to see that I had missed that critical moment, and that I would lose yet another windshield.

As the days passed, the little chip grew into a long line that made its way across my windshield. It moved so quickly, and the frosty, cold nights just aided its traveling speed. Every time I looked at the stupid line creeping across, I would become even more irritated.

Then something unexpected happened. God began using this situation to draw me closer to Him. I started thinking about how the crack was a good analogy for earthly distractions, worldly pursuits, or sin. I have come to learn that when the pleasures of this world are my focus, my actions usually fall quickly behind. Such actions often lead to some sort of sin, whether it is jealousy, pride, or other decisions that can have greater consequences. Just as I missed that crucial moment in time to get the chip fixed, neglecting these breaks in our connection with Christ can be quite similar. If it is not fixed by our Father right away, it can spreads like wildfire;

uncontrollably affecting our vision and the integrity of our being. It changes our perspective and even sometimes, we choose to change our beliefs to make ourselves comfortable with the way we are living or the decisions we are making. It can easily distort and destroy the things which we hold dear and that have eternal value in our lives, such as the people we love and are called to walk through this life with.

With my vehicle, the chip wasn't even noticeable until it spread further, creating more damage. Do we sometimes have sin in our lives that we have become so accustomed to, it isn't even recognizable? Until it spreads out of control, seeping further into our lives? How long are we willing to leave our sin unattended before we invite Christ into the broken pieces to fix and to heal?

> *How long are we willing to leave our sin unattended before we invite Christ into the broken pieces to fix and to heal?*

Just as the crack in my windshield weaved and turned, creating the most destruction possible, Satan will weave, confuse, and distort things to create the most destruction possible in our lives. This is how we create circumstances that are filled with anger, bitterness, confusion, worry, doubt, and brokenness. We need to tend to our soul wounds immediately to avoid these destruction-filled paths.

If I were to have noticed the crack the moment it was created, I would have been able to fix it almost back to its original state and integrity. It wouldn't have had the chance to spread and make a mess of my beautiful view. When we walk in an unbroken connection with the Holy Spirit, we are brought back to the important truths that guide us. We are able to catch those lies and distortions at the beginning before they have a chance to permeate our lives. The same goes with our sin; if we acknowledge it and repent immediately, it does not have the same power to creep into other aspects of our lives or hurt other people.

For a while, I chose to embrace this crack; partly because I didn't want to spend any more money on windshields, but it also reminded me to keep in unbroken connection with God, making sure there are no rock chips in the windshield of my life. Every time my eyes were drawn to the crack, I was reminded to check my heart, seek to abide in Christ, and hopefully react to daily circumstances in a Christ-like way. Next time your windshield cracks, use it as a reminder to check the integrity of your heart. Stay in constant connection with Him and don't let those cracks of sin seep further into your life.

The Bible also warns us of dangers of not dealing with sin. Proverbs 28:13 says, *"Whoever conceals their sins does not prosper, but the one who confesses and renounces them finds mercy."* Hiding our sin can be another hindrance to our goal to having an unbroken connection. But confessing our sins exposes it, which then allows for our spiritual connection to be restored. 1 John 1:9 promises us that *"If we confess our sins, He is faithful and just and will forgive us our sins and purify us from all unrighteousness."*

Often, we can feel so discouraged about an area where we struggle. It is so easy to feel defeated to the point where we don't even have that desire to pray or confess. But there is a blessing and reward in doing so. The power of the Holy Spirit gives us the strength to come back into connection with Him. Living in an unbroken connection with Him is more satisfying than any momentary pleasure we can aspire to experience here on earth. I say all of this from a place of grace. This isn't meant to be a guilt-trip, but a heart-check to see how we function day to day, and where our priorities lie.

This reality of wholeness, devotion, and an undivided heart is what we are looking for in order to experience spiritual sustenance through Christ. Some of us grew up with a legalistic mindset of rules and expectations that must be met in order to be "right with God." I want to reiterate the importance of our intimate friendship with Jesus, rather than serving some impersonal and detached deity. Our sustenance comes from our Saviour who walks with us each and every day. His grace is sufficient for every single one of us.

The power of the
Holy Spirit gives us the
strength to come back into
connection with Him.

# Exchanging Fear for Sustaining Faith

*Let us fix our eyes on Jesus, the author and perfecter of our faith. For the sake of the joy that lay before Him, He endured the cross, ignoring its shame, and is now seated at the right hand of the throne of God.*

*– Hebrews 12:2*

The culmination of faith and hope is critical to a joy-filled, Christian life. It's almost impossible to have hope that is not built on faith. For me, hope is the confident expectation that good is coming based on the promises of God. However, faith is a little different. It requires believing in God's promises and trusting in His faithfulness, which allows us to place our faith and reliance on

God's character to act; bringing things into order and providing resolution. Hebrews 11:1 states that, *"Now faith is confidence in what we hope for and assurance about what we do not see."* I believe one is built off of the other. I look at it as hope is believing that He can; faith is the anticipation of knowing He will and trusting Him to act in our lives. Our faith in Him is a direct result of who we believe Him to be. Pecorino (2005) stated that *"Faith is a necessary condition for hope: that no one can have hope without faith."*[1]

When we live in fear, we have chosen not to believe the Lord's promises and provision over our lives. This is the opposite of living in faith. Fear can cause a variety of feelings and be experienced in many different ways. Our fears can relate to social pressures, such as needing acceptance or approval. Fear can manifest as a phobia or a feeling of being unprotected, and often comes as a crippling companion to worry. When we live in fear, we are forsaking abiding in a supernatural faith that provides comfort above and beyond what the world can provide. When we function within the realm of the supernatural, we can experience peace from the Holy Spirit that can carry and calm us.

J.K. Rowling coined the phrase, *"Worrying means you suffer twice."*[2] The meaning behind it is implied; when you worry, you are creating stress before you even have to deal with a problem. Then, when the problem actually comes, you have to figure it out all over again. In fact, some of the big things that we waste our time worrying about never actually come to fruition. In either case, you are not benefiting yourself by worrying. Worrying brings about fear of the unknown or the future.

1. Philip A Pecorino, "Philosophy of Religion," The Interrelation of Faith and Hope, 2005, https://www.qcc.cuny.edu/social-sciences/ppecorino/phil_of_religion_text/chapter_10_definition/Faith-Hope.htm, 88.

2. Rowling, J K, and Scholastic Inc. 2016. Fantastic Beasts and Where to Find Them: Poster Book. New York, Ny: Scholastic, Inc.

Every type of fear is difficult for our entire being. I have struggled with fear in all its forms and I have learned that no matter how it presents itself, it is crippling; draining the life from within you. But let's take a moment to focus on the state we put ourselves in, as a result of choosing to walk day by day with fear as our closest companion. The following thoughts have created paralyzing storms of fear in my mind, robbing me of joy and contentment in my current state. Such thoughts only lead to turmoil and despair.

I have lived more than half of my life on my own. Several years ago, there were times I would sink into despair just by thinking,

If something happens to me in my house and I need assistance, who will even know something is wrong? I'm alone. How long would I be there before someone would find me?

Will I ever find a man that will choose me, love me, marry me, and will I have the opportunity to journey through this life with someone? On the flip side, if I don't find someone, will I be alone for the rest of my life? Am I okay with that?

As a single parent, do I have what it takes to parent my daughter well and be a godly influence in her life, drawing her closer to Jesus? Will she continue to follow Jesus when she is an adult? Will she resent me for not providing her with an earthly father? Will I be able to financially take care of us over the coming years?

I have taken note of the fact that when I am in a state of worry, my thinking most often revolves around myself. That's a quick cue to check my heart and perspective. Is my mindset an eternal or earthly one? A kingdom perspective revolves around mindsets that empower and encourage, giving hope and helping to align my mind with my maker's heart. Things that matter in an earthly mindset do not have the same weight in an eternal one.

To live focused on myself and meeting my needs is depressing, discouraging, and hopeless. So what counteracts fear? I think it is a mixture of things, especially when we take into account who is with us and acting on our behalf. The ability to rebuke fear is built on a foundation of faith in Jesus and knowing He is ultimately in control. However, I also think these other components function within your faith and will help you not live with the incessant presence of fear.

From my own experience, stepping back and accepting your current situation is key to reducing your fear. By that, I mean actually acknowledging it rather than planning how you are going to power through the unforeseen plans, or resign yourself to remaining in a season of struggle, with the bitterness that plans didn't unfold how and when you thought they should. Your timeline is not God's timeline. When we accept what our current circumstances are, this can lead to contentment as well as curiosity once we see the good in the unexpected. I would encourage this perspective when we consider our unmet longings. I am in no way implying that if someone is in a dangerous or unhealthy circumstance, they should just accept it. I am talking about when there is an ache in your heart because life just isn't unfolding how you thought it would.

*"Don't worry about anything; instead, pray about everything. Tell God what you need, and thank Him for all He has done"* (Philippians 4:6, NLT). Even when we don't understand our present circumstances, if we can have faith in God and wait for His will

*From this place of faith, hope can let you experience feelings of trust between you and your heavenly Father and safety in His purpose, plan, and love for you.*

to unfold, we are guaranteed a better ending because it is His divine plan, created for our good. This leads back to a biblical and faithful understanding of our Saviour. We must have the mind of Christ to combat the ever-present opportunities to partner with worry and fear! When we can stay in a place of security through faith, everything seems less frightening. You might even sense a bit of hope! From this place of faith, hope can let you experience feelings of trust between you and your heavenly Father and safety in His purpose, plan, and love for you.

I am not able to control everything that life throws at me, and the good news is that I don't have to. If I am ever faced with some of these challenges, I know God will give me strength at the time when I need it most. As Hebrews 4:16 states, *"Let us then with confidence draw near to the throne of grace, that we may receive mercy and find grace to help in time of need"* (ESV). So when I hear those fearful thoughts dangling in my mind, I will stop and give them back to God, declaring, no matter how it looks, you will sustain me, Jesus.

In her book, Victorious Emotions, Wendy Buckland states, *"Faith is not being in denial of the facts. It is having an ability to see the facts through the reality of God's faithfulness and supernatural ability to perform what He has promised."*[3] Now, there is some wisdom!

I have an overactive imagination and have to be careful what I put into my brain so that my mind doesn't wander in the darkness. I have lost peace and literally countless hours of sleep over the

---

3. Backlund, Wendy. 2017. Victorious Emotions.

years because of my wandering mind. I have learned how to cope with and see the life-giving or life-draining consequences of my choices. This includes the outcome from which thoughts I entertain too. What are the things you keep repeating to yourself? Are they hope-filled or heartbroken? Are they centered on the joy of your faith? Or are they wallowing with doubt from your prior experiences? It's incredibly easy to stay there, but it is a hard path to trudge alone.

I have lived long enough on this earth to see so much heartache and pain. It makes me long for my home in heaven. You don't have to look very far to see injustice or the pain of trauma and heartbreak around us due to addictions, abuse, divorce, disease, death, and relational turmoil. It is so easy to develop a fear of experiencing pain and heartache just by living life. There were times when it felt like I was continually bracing myself for the next hardship. Living in this place of constant fear for the next blow to my heart or trial to trudge was an exhausting way to live.

> *God wants us to be present with Him today and not be overly focused on what lies ahead down the road: a day, a week, a year, or a decade.*

I love this one translation of Matthew 6:34 by The Message. It says, *"Give your entire attention to what God is doing right now, and don't get worked up about what may or may not happen tomorrow. God will help you deal with whatever hard things come up when the time comes."* It's not a suggestion but more of a command.

God wants us to be present with Him today and not be overly focused on what lies ahead down the road: a day, a week, a year, or a decade. We aren't even guaranteed that time! Instead, we must be present and focused on what is in front of us and how He is sustaining us right now.

Peace is a spiritual blessing that can overtake any fear or worry we experience. Faith is not the absence of fear, but the hope that perseveres through the trials and unknowns of life. I think John Eldredge and Brent Curtis said it best when they stated, *"Faith looks back and draws courage; hope looks ahead, and keeps desire alive."*[4] In this world so full of disappointments and unknowns, we must have faith. We must choose when we feel weakened by the weight of life to dig deep and stand firm in our faith.

---

4. Eldredge, John, and Brent Curtis. 2008. The Sacred Romance. Nashville: Thomas Nelson, C.

We must be present and focused on what is in front of us and how He is sustaining us right now.

# Exchanging Brokenness for Sustaining Hope

*So do not fear, for I am with you; do not be dismayed, for I am your God. I will strengthen you and help you; I will uphold you with my righteous right hand.*

*– Isaiah 41:10*

Hope is like a muscle. It needs to be used to build strength. Even when we have a strong foundation in our faith, where we know to trust God's character and His word, life can still have a way of wrecking us. I know it has for me over the years. There have been some heartaches in my life that rattled and wrecked my hope while my faith was still intact. Maybe I had some questions about God's plan or timing, but I still knew God was God. There was no question for me about His presence and His deity.

When it comes to hope, a common problem that we can fall into is that we make up our own timeline of how life is going to unfold. We don't seek God to find out what He has for us. We don't give our life over to His plan and purpose. We decide how it's all going to go. Today, we are bombarded with messages to "follow your heart": a terrible idea. Jeremiah 17:9 tells us *"The heart is deceitful above all things and beyond cure. Who can understand it?"* Trust me, don't follow your heart! Our society aims to empower everyone to choose whatever makes them happy, at any cost. When we look at Scripture, that is the exact opposite of what God calls us to do. Blindly following your heart leads to destruction.

Given that we are bombarded with messages about how life should unfold and what will make us happy, it doesn't take long for us to conjure up our own ideas independent of God. We have the job, marriage, babies, and retirement plans all figured out and anticipate that it will all go Bibbidi-Bobbidi-Boo and fall into place. So let me ask: what part of your life isn't going as you originally planned? How have you been at accepting that? If you feel like your own plans lay in shattered scraps, you're not alone. For most people I interact with, even if there is so much good in their lives, they can acknowledge, there is usually at least one part of their life that hasn't panned out as they anticipated. For some, it seems like they have been dealt blow after blow. These people are some of the strongest believers I know. I admire them deeply. I am not wanting to focus on the one bad thing amidst the countless blessings, but I want to acknowledge the hurt that someone can face when their hope has been deferred in an area. It is painful.

I had hardships as a child and felt the pain of living on this earth. I realized very early that this life wasn't going to be a fairytale, but I still chose to hope. Just before my twentieth birthday is when it all imploded, and I had to pick up the pieces. The agony first hit me when the man I was engaged to suddenly got cold feet. He didn't have the life experience to handle how he was feeling or the ability to process his thoughts with anyone, so he shattered my heart in a phone call. I have never been so blindsided as in that moment. His confusion led him to a place of indecision, and I was shocked and in agony waiting for him to decide whether he still wanted to be with me.

God graciously helped us navigate through the situation and in the end, we called off our wedding less than three months before our wedding date. I was young and in love. I had gone into the engagement with honourable intentions and high hopes. I was naive and thought this was my fairy tale ending. It ended before it began and it crushed me. The hardest part was that I had jumped in, shared all my hopes and desires, and started planning a life with this man. The dreams and longings that I had associated with a wedding, and life as a mother and wife, came alive with him as we spoke them into existence through our planning. When the engagement ended, along with the plans for our future together, the time spent dreaming felt like such a waste to me. They became tainted memories, and I didn't want those dreams anymore. But since I had shared them all with him, I had nothing left. My hope of marrying, being a wife, and being a mother had been obliterated.

To add to the heartbreak was an embarrassment, as I had a planned wedding that had to be canceled. Some moments reiterated just how painful it all could be: calling back the flower shop to cancel the flower arrangements; having my parents pick up my beautiful wedding dress and hide it in a closet so I didn't have to face it; feeling awkward and embarrassed at the shock in peoples' faces when they would come to congratulate me, but instead consoled me. Worst of all, was the lack of emotion and empathy that this man I loved seemed to have towards the situation at the time and saying goodbye to me, or at least that's how I perceived it. The person I had planned to spend my life with left my life completely in the blink of an eye. It was brutal.

Rejection will always gnaw away at your sense of self-worth. Consequently, I had to reframe my purpose and worth by truly seeking God, listening to Him, and discovering what He actually had planned for my life. Those years of expectation, Disney princesses being rescued and true love's kiss making everything perfect, didn't fade so easily. I mourned the hope of those dreams in my heart. I felt betrayed by the idea of love itself. Now all I knew is that loving someone was a surefire ingredient to providing the most pain you could ever experience....when you lose them, or worse yet when they decide they don't want you anymore.

We broke up in July and as September came, I couldn't even fathom being able to go back to our university and see his face. I contemplated enrolling somewhere else, but my father, in one of his most confident and loving moments toward his daughter, encouraged me to go back to school with my head held high and continue the dreams I had to become a teacher. So I did. I made it through each day, feeling nauseous when our paths crossed. I held myself together, and when I returned to the safety of my vehicle, I would cry all the way home.

It left me with feelings of rejection, worthlessness, and shame. It rattled my confidence in this concept of love and a heavenly Father who had good plans for my life. How had I got it all so wrong? Life wasn't going to turn out the way I had planned. That's when fear and hopelessness barged in and made a comfy little nest within Julianna's soul.

It's important to note that after a decade and a half later, I am thankful that we didn't get married, and I hold no bitterness toward the situation or the people involved. We were two young people figuring out life and love and ended up hurting each other in the process. Although this is my perspective of how things went, I am sure there are things I did that hurt him as well. I know that my desire for my fairy tale ending placed him up on a pedestal with a lot of expectations, and no one is meant to have to carry all that on their own. No one person can solely sustain another; that's what Jesus is for. I bless him and wish him and his family joy, health, and an abundance of God's favour in their lives.

If I had to pinpoint where I had a crisis of hope, that's when it happened! I don't think I realized it at the time, but it was that moment in time when I had to choose what path I was going to take. The first path remained close to Jesus, finding refuge in Him because of the rattled hope that encompassed my entire perspective of life. The second path questioned and doubted God's goodness because of my rattled hope. Looking back, I think I hung in the balance between the two for so long. I didn't blatantly deny or try to defy God, but He also didn't seem

*In my mind, a lack of hope meant a lack of hurt. What I came to find out is that abandoning hope simply causes heartache in other ways.*

safe to me at the time. It no longer seemed safe to hope.
I planned and adjusted my future to something I thought I could control, which was pursuing my career as a teacher, as well as my love for travel. In my mind, a lack of hope meant a lack of hurt. What I came to find out is that abandoning hope simply causes heartache in other ways.

But God is gracious, and although I had created distance, He was still there, pursuing me and protecting me, in the darkness, in the deceit, in the defiance. I am so thankful He saw my heart amidst the pain and loved me regardless of my choices. Regrettably, it ended up taking more pain and heartache for me to realize that my own plan was an even worse idea and that my own choices led me to even worse places. It wasn't until I was totally broken and desperate to be saved that He gave me the strength to readjust my perspective again. This season of my life literally needs another book devoted to it. So you'll have to wait for that! Even though it was a scary time of my life, there was repentance and restoration and a desire to be hopeful again. I've had more crises of hope since this one, but with God's grace, I think they seem to be less detrimental each time because I have learned where I need to turn my eyes in those times: on Him. When our hearts are in alignment with God's will and direction, it can be a very beautiful thing.

How we choose to perceive life's events really affects our joy. Wendy Backlund put it this way: You can live a hope-filled life with a few disappointments or a hopeless life that is safe.... Which one will you choose today?[5]

When I read what she wrote about a perspective of hope, I reworded this for myself and pinned it up onto my hope board.

5. Backlund, Wendy. 2017. Victorious Emotions.

My eyes catch it as I get ready in the morning, and it helps me check my perspective.

When my two options are put into a statement like that, my choice seems very obvious. Why wouldn't I choose a life filled with hope, knowing that God is in control and has my best interests in mind? Yes, there will be disappointments; we live on earth and there is sin on earth. But with Jesus, I know that I can deal with the disappointments as they come. He will give me the grace to do so. So I choose a hope-filled life! I hope you choose that way too. Look back at the times God has been faithful to you and use that to draw hope for the things you are waiting for!

In my mind, a lack of hope meant a lack of hurt. What I came to find out is that abandoning hope simply causes heartache in other ways.

# Exchanging Longings for Sustaining Contentment

*For the LORD God is a sun and shield; the LORD bestows favor and honor; no good thing does he withhold from those whose walk is blameless.*

*- Psalm 84:11*

*"Hope deferred makes the heart sick, but a longing fulfilled is a tree of life"* (Proverbs 13:12). I remember the first time my eyes found this verse in the Bible. I was almost annoyed. My friend quoted it to me after I poured out my heart one day to her about some of my unmet longings. I didn't know this wisdom was in the Bible regarding my unmet longings. It was like God was saying to me, "Well duh, of course you feel heartbroken!" At that time, I had a lot less understanding of God's sovereign plan over my life

and a whole lot more questions and anger with the way things had unfolded. However, something in finding the verse gave me comfort. It allowed me to know I wasn't crazy or delusional. It made sense why I felt so hopeless. I felt like so many hopeful situations in my life, or circumstances that at first brought hope and joy, did not play out the way I thought they would.

Surrendering your longings to Christ in the only way to find contentment throughout the waiting. Understanding this concept, regarding this personal type of surrender is a truth that I have learned in the last few years of my life. Sometimes, I can't believe it took me nearly thirty years to truly believe it, but it did. Even more embarrassing, I can still completely forget this truth and start questioning everything again, sending my thoughts into a negative spiral. It shows me something about the perspective I hold. It can be so easy to be so egocentric in our view of life and His plan, which is full of His goodness. Surrendering my will to His, and choosing to trust Him even when it does not make sense to me is something I am continually working at. Even though I've had breakthroughs with this concept of submission, it seems so easy to forget when my emotions make me feel otherwise. That is why we must not follow our emotions but let the Bible lead our hearts to the truth.

At first, I was shocked by all the things I had to say and stories I had to share about this struggle with longings and finding contentment. After reflection, it now makes sense. Living with contentment in the midst of unmet longings is an area that I have struggled with the longest and likely the most. Jesus has reminded me that it's okay to be honest. We have different seasons in our lives and sometimes we are stronger in one area at one time than another. So, I ask you to be gracious and see that I am also still learning to trust the father faithfully in my journey. Maybe you'll find some of your own tendencies here. I hope you can find a nugget of truth as you read to encourage your heart.

In Psalm 84:11 it says, *"The Lord gives grace and glory; He withholds no good thing from those whose walk is blameless."* I remember the day that I first truly believed this beautiful statement. It was back in February 2018; I was in California with my best friend. During the worship portion of a church service, the worship leader said, *"The Father does not withhold good things from us!"* She repeated that phrase a few times in between songs. She said it with hope, peace, and conviction in her voice. I don't even remember what she said after that because those words pierced through my heart. I started crying. I am sure I had heard some similar phrasing of this between my family and friends over my lifetime, but it never sank in.

Within five seconds, my perspective of God's goodness changed forever. It addressed a misconception I had about Him and His plans for me. I realized that up until that moment, I never thought of my waiting in life in this way. I was resentful and confused, and part of me did think God was withholding good things from me, like marriage and children. I had been confused, bitter, and sometimes just fed up about it. Why did He create in me these desires just to leave them unfulfilled? It felt cruel.

At that moment, I realized my Father had not been withholding these good things from me, but that things had not come into alignment yet. Some aspects of the equation weren't ready, and it just was not at a place where it could mold together to be a good thing. Therefore, it hadn't happened yet. It just wouldn't be a good thing for me.... YET! I was able to see God differently, and I felt a new realization that was mostly peace mixed with a new-found hope. I realized I had resentment about these questions and was withholding pursuit in some aspects of my own relationship with Jesus because I didn't understand the waiting. But as the revelation of His goodness and timing became clearer, a part of my heart softened.

Another part of my heart became hopeful. They say, *"Faith in God includes faith in His timing"*[6] and that's the part where my planner, logical brain struggles. However, if I lean into Him and trust that He has my best interests in mind, then I can have peace with the unknown. Something in me changed that day. I think about that phrase often, and it continues to give me hope and affirm that my God is for me.

Years later, I still do not have an answer about my singleness. I don't know if this longing will be fulfilled in the way I anticipate. Since I trust that God is not withholding good things from me now, it doesn't bother me the way it used to. I try to hold the desire open-handed, giving it to God. I trust that whatever the outcome, it is what is best for me. I might not ever know why until I get to heaven, yet my trust in Him is enough while I wait for the answers.

> *I trust that whatever the outcome, it is what is best for me. I might not ever know why until I get to heaven, yet my trust in Him is enough while I wait for the answers.*

It was such a breakthrough for me that I painted Psalm 84:11 on a plaque. It hangs in my bedroom as a constant reminder. The promise behind the words is what gives my heart peace, and I wanted the reminder of the revelation.

---

6. Maxwell, Neal. 1991. "Lest Ye Be Wearied and Faint in Your Minds." In .

If something isn't happening in my life, it is not because God doesn't want to give me good things. It's because it isn't a good thing for me, or He has something much better planned. I just need to chill out and trust Him! The logical part of me wants more of an explanation than that, but that is where faith comes in.

Now I think I would be remiss if I didn't take a moment to focus on the last part of the verse, ...to those whose walk is blameless. Another way of phrasing it would be, to those who live with integrity. I think it is important that this is a truth we can count on when we are aligning ourselves with His truth and living in a way that is God honouring. This isn't to say we will not mess up and make mistakes. We are all working out our salvation and becoming like Jesus and it doesn't happen overnight. As believers, He sees us as saints- as His children, as redeemed by the blood of Jesus. So, although we are still capable of sin, we are no longer sinners. We all fall; it's all about the comeback!

If you don't personally know Jesus, the idea of receiving certain blessings based on walking in integrity may sound intimidating or even overwhelming. Once you realize that the gift of salvation gives you the freedom to be seen through the righteousness of Christ, it changes everything. You don't have to strive for perfection anymore; you are already enough. You are whole not because of anything that you have done or accomplished, but it's His identity that covers you and that's how the Creator now sees you. It's complex, but the new identity that we are given when receiving His sweet salvation, free from condemnation and shame of our past, is the most beautiful gift that can ever be given to us. It's given out of love. If you haven't experienced this gift, all that is required is recognition that you are a sinner who needs the grace of Jesus;

to realize that He loved you so much and that He died for you on the cross to atone for your sins. Ask Him to become the Lord of your life and see the beautiful change that commences. When you live from this place, the idea of walking in integrity is much more achievable because you aren't doing it on your own.

My personal hope for walking with integrity is proven in the life of King David. He was known as a man after God's own heart. It is clear that God loved him and had wonderful plans for his life, yet David messed up all the time. Even more so, because in the world's eyes, he messed up in huge ways.... murder, adultery, the list goes on...

I love to see how he always came back to God! David did have to face consequences for his choices but in the end, God still worked it all out for his good. I am so thankful that we serve a good God. I know in my own life when I have chosen to go my own way, to try to make things happen for myself because I didn't like God's timing, it has only ended in heartbreak and disaster. Thankfully, God has been so gracious and forgiving, and I have learned from those experiences. But oh boy, it was not worth it at all. At times when I feel frustrated by the way life is going, I have asked God to remind me of the path I was on and the pain it caused, because it is the most excellent reminder to not choose my own path again.

I have the perfect example of God's amazing timing in my own life and how the waiting was so worth it! It is a reminder of His faithfulness, and I can't help but be encouraged in my faith when I reflect upon it. I hope it will do the same for you! When I decided to adopt as a single woman, I was excited! God had shown me that this was something I could do on my own. Why wait to be married to love a child in need? So I jumped in with both feet! Over the five years that I waited, I fostered many different children. On three separate occasions, I inquired about adopting those sweet little girls. I was fostering them in some manner, knew them very well, and was currently meeting their needs. Each time, my worker would come back with an answer stating that due to their unique circumstances and needs and my eligibility as a single applicant, their needs would be too high for me to handle on their own; every time was a resounding no.

I was confused and frustrated at times because I knew the child and had spent time with them. I knew I could have been a mother to them and didn't understand why it wouldn't have worked. Logically, it didn't add up to me. My worker once replied with a no but encouraged me by saying that they hadn't forgotten about me. Looking back, she sent this email to me, with the knowledge that they were currently in the process of matching my future daughter with me. She knew what was coming, but I had no idea. I wonder about the anticipation she felt as she crafted that email to me, knowing there was a hopeful foreshadowing of the near future.

One Friday night in May 2018, when I was earnestly seeking contentment with Jesus, I gave it all back to Him. I sat in my backyard until it was completely dark. I looked up at the stars and told Jesus that if this was all there ever was- if it was just going to be me and Him- I'd be happy with that! It was something that I needed to do, and it required bravery at that moment. I know I was sincere, and I felt the peace of Jesus over my heart. I was content even though my longings weren't yet fulfilled. I knew God would open and close doors as he planned, and I left that in His hands.

We all know that God works in mysterious ways. That was on

a Friday night. Three days later on Monday while I was at work, I received a phone call. My worker told me that she had a match for me. We planned a meeting as soon as possible. I remember running down the hall to find my best friend to tell her the amazing news. I completely interrupted her class, pulled her into the hallway, and our eyes both filled with joyful tears as I told her what had just unfolded.

What I didn't know was that there was this sweet little girl who Jesus had waiting for me whom I had never met before. We went through the meetings, and God made it so clear that this was His plan. I excitedly agreed and we were matched. I got to meet her the following week. I've never felt so excited and nervous at the same time. How does someone prepare for this moment?

The first time I met her, she came down the concrete path of her foster home with a crimson Gerber daisy in her hand. She walked up to me, gave me the flower, and called me Mom. It was surreal, yet so natural. When I first heard her infectious laughter as I pushed her on the glider, I was enchanted. All I wanted was more. Within three weeks of meeting her, she moved in with me and our life together began. It has only gotten better as we keep going! What joy it brings a parent to see their child flourish and excel; to reflect Jesus' love in her words and actions. The Lord uses her to humble me and to remind me of what really matters; drawing me back to a kingdom perspective.

The more I came to know her, the more baffled I was about us being brought together. The people in our lives that have the privilege of knowing her, know that we are two peas in a pod. We both love adventure and being silly! There's nothing like that twinkle in her eye when she knows she's going to make me laugh with her next antic. We both love to explore, we love to sing, and have a shared sense of ridiculous humour. We are both very social and enjoy a good adrenaline rush. Our personalities fit so well. She is perfectly matched with me, and I like to think the reciprocal of that is also true. I aim to be a complement to her, in meeting her needs and knowing her heart; I can attest to her being mine.

In our first four years of life together, we have had beautiful memories, filled with laughter, adventure, and a bond that assures me that this was God's best for both of us. It required waiting. It wasn't my first option. It wasn't even an option I knew I wanted or even specifically pursued. But God knew all along... in the midst of waiting, the no's made no sense. Now, after seeing His plan unfold, I can only praise Him for a plan that is far better than anything I could have ever orchestrated. My heart rejoices. She is so joyful and brings joy to my soul as I watch her learn to love God and grow and excel. She's a little walking miracle, and I am beyond blessed to be the one chosen to guide her through life.

*He has taught me to be thankful for His no's because I can be expectant that He has a better yes.*

When I think about those other little girls, I pray for them and hope they found a wonderful home. I am thankful that God shut those doors for me at the time and for the years of waiting so that He could bring my daughter to be with me. For me, it is an undeniable story. He has taught me to be thankful for His no's because I can be expectant that He has a better yes. His way is always better than anything I could conjure up!

About a year ago, I came across a quote that was life-changing for me: *"Love ceases to be a demon only when it ceases to be a god."*[7] The inverse then would also be true that love becomes a demon when it becomes a god. When I read it, I instantly stopped to reread it and take it in. I knew that it would be one that would be used in the future to quickly tune my heart to a kingdom perspective. I immediately wrote this quote down on a sticky note and stuck it to my hope board. For me, this quote is talking about romantic love and idolization that the world has given in. For so long, it was my argument that if love wasn't such a wonderful thing, then why does almost every movie contain a love story? Why do most songs have to somehow connect with romantic love or lack thereof? I have learned and changed my thinking to understand that just because romantic love is the focus of the world, it does not give it the same weight in the kingdom of God.

Now before anyone gets offended, I am not saying that romantic love and marriage are bad. I know they are a beautiful gift. I am talking about the idolization of romantic love to the point where our happiness, purpose, and value are centered around whether we find this everlasting earthly love that is supposed to fill every void and insecurity, forever and ever amen. That's not what God designed marriage to look like, and the minute we idolize it to that level and put that type of pressure on another human, who also sins and has struggles, is when we lose perspective.

So would I love to experience a healthy, romantic love on this earth? Of course! But I check my mindset often. The absence of romance does not change my value, purpose, or ability to experience joy. Too many people believe that they need a romantic partner to be fulfilled. It is a lie that creates in them a sense of

---

7. Lewis, C S. (1960) 1960. The Four Loves. San Francisco: Harperone.

hopelessness or a lack of worth. Today is one of those days when I find myself questioning what God is doing with my life. There is still definitely more trust in Him, but again, things are unfolding differently than the way I foresaw. Good old expectations, eh? I live far away from my family and see them during vacations; not as much as I'd like to but am so thankful for the time we have together. The distance causes me to sometimes question why I am still living so far away. Frequently, I feel lonely and wish for a companion to walk through this life with and someone to co-parent with, although I've heard that's no walk in the park either. Often, my daughter expresses her desire about having siblings or a dad and has questions that I do not have answers to. It's not easy being a single mom. Regularly, my prayers consist of me stating my frustrations to the Lord saying things like, I don't get it God! or Please give her a wonderful father! or Why can't you allow this good desire for a husband and father to be fulfilled?

Then He gently reminds me of our story, and I can't help but have faith in His plan. Every night before bed, I pray over my sweet baby girl and thank God for the good plans He has for her life. I want her to hear that over and over again and believe it! When she asks about a daddy or brothers or sisters, I tell her the same thing I tell myself: *"God loves us. He has good plans for our lives. We can tell Him how we feel, and it's okay to ask Him questions, but we need to trust Him. He has the best plan for us!"*

His will and timing are always best. I truly don't know what our future holds. Maybe it will include some lucky man who gets two for the price of one and becomes a husband and instant father. Let me tell you, we are a good time! He would be blessed just to be her dad! But maybe it will just be the two of us. I know if that happens

He will sustain us, and we will still have an abundant and joy-filled life. For reasons I may not know and understand on this earth, that will be His best for us, and He will give me the heart and faith to trust that. He has already filled our lives with such wonderful people, and we have already had so many wonderful experiences together. I see Him taking care of us! I know that if I trust God with whatever our future holds, it will be what is best for us, and that's all I need to know for now.

I don't know what you're waiting for, but I can empathize with you. I understand the fine line we are walking here when it comes to waiting and hoping. Sometimes it seems easier to build a safe environment where you just focus on what you know, forget about desires, and do not hope for something because hoping opens the possibility for pain. This is something my heart is often tempted to do. It allows me to feel more stable and more in control.

What I can tell you is that I keep a much better perspective when I remain close to Jesus; when I'm in the Word, reading good books, and filling my head with songs that draw me to Him and His goodness. That's not to say that my daughter and I don't enjoy jamming out to Tina Turner weekly in the kitchen. I think God smiles down on us in those moments too. When I fill my mind and time with other things, it doesn't go so well, which is when He gently uses those spiraling thoughts as a reminder to come back. What I want you to understand is that God is not withholding good things from coming into your life! Having faith when it seems impossible to see your desired outcome can be really challenging. I know I was all positive earlier, but trust me, I still have my moments of doubt. I am a work in progress. I also don't have all the answers and I know I never will. But He does. That is what makes

Him God! Trusting our Father with the longings in our heart is how we persevere. Knowing that, in many cases, He gave us those desires and wants to fulfill them is what allows us to submit to His will and timing, knowing it is best. When we align our hearts and mind to Him, surrendering to His will, we experience a contentment that no other source can offer.

When we align our hearts and mind to Him, surrendering to His will, we experience a contentment that no other source can offer.

_____

# Exchanging Loneliness for Sustaining Security

*The LORD your God is with you, the Mighty Warrior who saves. He will take great delight in you; in His love He will no longer rebuke you, but will rejoice over you with singing.*
*- Zephaniah 3:17*

Loneliness is something that I have fought against my entire life. Sure, I have moments where I am content with my singleness and the life that I have built. While I am humble enough to see that God has given me the blessings in this life, in many ways I feel like I have built it on my own. I have spent a lot of my life on my own and learning to enjoy my own company, while also pursuing the presence of my Saviour. John Eldredge stated in his book, The Sacred Romance, *"We are made in the image of God; we carry within us the desire for our true life of intimacy and adventure. To say we want less than that is to lie."*[8] I couldn't agree more.

However, I have learned over the years that loneliness can be a gift. God can use it to draw us closer to Him, to rely on Him in other ways we might not naturally do if we weren't lonely. Max Lucado gave a wonderful illustration of the gift of loneliness in his book, Traveling Light. He explains that we misunderstand the idea of loneliness. It is not the absence of people in our lives, but the absence of intimacy within our relationships[9]. Loneliness is not the physical reality of being alone, but believing we are alone and having to face the hardships of our life on our own.

Lucado (2003) suggests that instead of running from the feeling of loneliness, and despising it, we should embrace it; seeing what it has to offer us. This is where he introduces the concept of the gift of loneliness. He explains that God can sometimes use our solitude to grab our attention. He uses an illustration of going on a long trip, with the anticipation of listening to your favourite music on the way. To modernize his illustration, imagine you have the entire vibe of the drive planned out with your highly anticipated playlist queued up. Unfortunately, the playlist you selected isn't downloaded on your phone and you end up in an area without cell service, so you lose access to the songs. On your way to your destination, you pick up your friend. You haven't seen them in a while so you are a little apprehensive about how your time driving will unfold. However, your always-prepared friend has their playlists downloaded on their phone and available to listen to. They don't listen to the same type of music you do, but you allow them to play their music since you

8. Eldredge, John, and Brent Curtis. 2008. The Sacred Romance. Nashville: Thomas Nelson, C.
9. Lucado, Max. 2003. Traveling Light. Waterville, Maine Thorndike Press.

have no other option. At first, you aren't sure of these new artists and styles of music, but as the hours pass, you come to appreciate these new discoveries of music. You might even add some of them to your own playlists when you get back to your destination.

Through this series of events, you become exposed to artists and songs that you didn't know even existed, nor could you foretell that you would enjoy them. What led to this discovery of your newfound appreciation and enjoyment of this music? It's not something you would have chosen on your own, but since you were out of options, you became open to the idea of something else other than what you initially had planned for on this road trip.

God wants you to hear His music. In order for you to appreciate what He has to offer, He has to get rid of the other distractions that you were previously drawn to. Lucado uses this to exemplify the noise of life and the things you chase. God can use loneliness to quiet the distractions one has in their life so that they can then hear His voice. Through time spent with Him, you will develop an intimacy and appreciation of His voice that will provide fresh revelation of His love for you. This can change your perceptions of yourself, your plans, and perhaps, even your hopes and desired outcomes during a particular season of your life. I have seen this unfold in my own life.

One critical aspect of loneliness, which has the potential to be detrimental to us, is the choices we make in our attempt to escape our loneliness. If we are not wise, we can easily create an even worse type of pain than just loneliness. Sometimes, the fear of being lonely drives us to make choices that aren't in our best interest. Lucado (2003) suggests that, *"For fear of not fitting in, we take the drugs......for fear of going unnoticed, we dress to seduce or to impress. For fear of sleeping alone, we sleep with anyone. For fear of not being loved, we search for love in all the wrong places."*

Thankfully, once we discover God's unconditional love for us, His perfect love casts out fear (1 John 4:18). Once we are confident in His love for us, we are no longer desperately seeking love from others. It gives us godly confidence and freedom that can't be experienced from any other source.

Lucado (2003) ends this illustration with the question, *"If a season of solitude is His way to teach you to hear His song, don't you think it's worth it?"* [10] As the church, I think we must look at the role of singleness and view it from a more positive standpoint. Rather than questioning what is wrong with someone for being older and still single, we need to understand that God's timing and path are different for each person. A single person's journey is just as important as a married person's journey. God can use each person, in their particular season, for His glory. Singleness can provide a person with a beautiful opportunity of experiencing God in a unique way, and knowing Him intimately; allowing Him to meet some of the longings in their heart that one might have placed on a romantic partner. I know it has been true for me.

> *Singleness can provide a person with a beautiful opportunity of experiencing God in a unique way, and knowing Him intimately*

I have been able to find blessings in my singleness. Jesus has used that time to grow and strengthen my relationship with Him when I felt most lonely. Since I was longing for connection, I was particularly eager to hear from Him. When I waited in that silence for Him and was met with His gentle words of affection and

---

10. Lucado, Max. 2003. Traveling Light. Waterville, Maine Thorndike Press.

affirmation for me, I couldn't help but be changed and empowered to live from a place of trust and contentment in my Saviour's sweet sustaining presence.

The Bible is full of promises of God's faithfulness and presence. Whether from the people we read about throughout the Bible, or coming directly from Jesus himself, these promises are declared time and again. David said, *"I am not alone. You go before me and follow me. You place your hand of blessing on my head"* (Psalm 139:5, NLT). The Lord told the Israelites, *"So do not fear, for I am with you; do not be dismayed, for I am your God. I will strengthen you and help you. I will uphold you with my righteous right hand"* (Isaiah 41:10). David found confidence in God's provision declaring, "Even though I walk through the darkest valley, I will fear no evil, for you are with me; your rod and your staff, they comfort me." (Psalm 23:4). Lastly, one I have found solace in many times. Psalm 34:18 reminds us that *"The Lord is close to the brokenhearted and saves those who are crushed in spirit."*

While I acknowledge the way that God can use loneliness to our benefit in a certain season, I also believe He created us for community. We aren't meant to go through this life alone. God doesn't want that for us. He provides us with people to walk with along the journey. That can come in the form of many different types of relationships. This is something that Jesus has shown me many times, particularly in a season when I was intent on pursuing Him. He was so gracious and showed His love in so many ways, which I understood as His pursuit of me. One of my biggest takeaways was that God has never asked me to walk this life alone. No, I don't have a husband but God has filled my life with beautiful relationships that constantly meet so many of my needs.

Over ten years ago, I left the only life I had known in Nova Scotia to move to Northern Alberta. I didn't know a single soul. I moved for an opportunity within my teaching career. In my move across the country, God blessed me with people to act like my adopted family. I've lived here for eleven years now and while some relationships were for a season(and they were so needed in those seasons), some relationships have lasted throughout my time here and have gotten richer with time. I have friends who meet my physical needs when things break down in the home and friends who come to my aid to take care of my daughter so I can have a night off. I have friends who provide me with hysterical laughter, friends who will comfort me, mourn with me, celebrate with me, friends to play games with, go camping with, and enjoy the subtle art of speaking with a British accent just for fun! I have even closer friends that challenge me spiritually and empower me to live with a bold faith and kingdom mindset focused on an eternal perspective rather than a fleeting, worldly perspective.

I am often overwhelmed by the richness I have in multiple relationships that meet different needs in my life. God showed me that He intends us to lean on others through life, to allow others to meet our needs. Yes, we need to focus on our relationship with Him, and He is the one who answers our prayers and provides for us, but He often uses others to be the ones who are our answers to prayers.

*I have been in this season of letting go of my expectations and longings for what a romantic relationship would be. This is not out of a loss of hope but out of contentment for this season of life, where I am enjoying the other relationships which God has so richly blessed me.*

I have been in this season of letting go of my expectations and longings for what a romantic relationship would be. This is not out of a loss of hope but out of contentment for this season of life, where I am enjoying the other relationships which God has so richly blessed me. I may not get flowers from a man, but I have had friends who have given me flowers and it has meant just as much in its own way because of the heart behind it.. Let me share a beautiful story of an encounter that is sweet evidence that God hears every prayer: even in those mundane moments, when your prayer comes out as a pathetic mumble rather than a coherent thought, as you are poorly fighting against self-pity.... but Jesus has grace for that too.

It was back in the spring of 2020, I had been through a rough few months and a particularly difficult week. I had torn a ligament in my knee skiing in Jasper a few months prior which was very painful. I had struggled to walk for months and missed an incredible amount of time teaching. I think I got back to school for about three days when I got sick with COVID and then was out for another three weeks. These situations created the scenario of spending months at home; out of my routine, alone, with too much time to think.

I missed my students terribly and felt guilty for missing so much work and not being as present as I wanted to be with my daughter amidst my pain. It was a hard time. To make matters worse at that particular time, I had ended a relationship with a man that just wasn't going to work out. I knew it was the right decision, but it was still very difficult; to let go of the hope of what could have been.

God has given me a very tender heart, one that cares easily. It's the same tenderness that has led me to adopt my beautiful daughter and invest in my students and friendships the way I do. Also, it is very difficult to say goodbye to that type of companionship, knowing it will not be quickly replaced. My head and my heart were in very different places. I am happy to say I followed my head and God's leading, but my heart was a mess.

With each burden piling on top of the other, my heart was weary. I was struggling to get through the days and keep it together for my daughter. I knew time would be a healer for this type of heartache, but my thoughts were really making it hard for me to put my decision in the past and feel truly hopeful for the future. Combined with the weight of the months prior, it felt like I was not getting a break and was merely surviving....

I had a few moments where I was at the grocery store and had the inclination to buy flowers for myself just as a boost for my heavy heart. Each time I pondered the idea and then decided no because the money could be put to better use or the thought that I shouldn't have to do that to feel better. I just wasn't giving myself too much grace for where my heart was. The day before, my daughter and I were at Walmart and I actually picked up a bouquet, smelt it, and admired the beautiful colours that created this masterpiece. The pink, purple, and white flowers were soft and subtle, but so beautiful. I was about to put it in the cart and decided to look at the price tag. I felt guilty again about spending $20 and put it back, deciding that was the final time I was going to ponder flowers. We then went and bought what we needed from the grocery section and headed home.

When I woke up one morning, I felt very low. As I watched in the mirror as my wand curled my hair, I saw myself holding in the tears. My heart was just not okay. It was heavy and it still had not caught up with my head in the decisions that I had made. With very little hope, I began to pray that God would change my heart, renew my mind, and help me get through this day; that I would focus on my daughter and my students and all I have to be grateful for. I ended with a pitiful plea that went something like this: God, if you could just show me that you are here right now, I need that. Please uniquely show me, so I know it's from you, that you are pursuing me and you love me. That was all I could muster up to pray. I chose to ask to be pursued by God. I knew I needed to pursue Jesus and draw near to Him but wanted to know He was pursuing me too.

The day went by and I found myself happily distracted by work and the clever, wittiness of my fifth-grade students. I came home, spent time with my daughter, and put her to bed. I was having trouble spending my nights alone and had been purposely developing new routines, so I had filled up my calendar with nightly visits, or phone calls with friends or my mom to just help pass the time. Thank goodness for those friends!

My sweet friend was coming over and texted to see what Starbucks drink I wanted. I put in my normal order for a Grand Chai Tea Latte. That in itself ministered to my heart. When she arrived, I opened up the door, and guess what else she had in her hands? A beautiful bouquet of purple, pink, and white flowers! I was overwhelmed with surprise and joy. I told her about my prayer and how many times I had wanted to buy myself flowers in the past week but hadn't done so. I noticed that the flowers looked identical to the ones I had picked up the day before from Walmart and inquired as to where she got them. She had picked them up at Walmart too! The exact same ones! That's not a coincidence, that is

Jesus and His sweet love.

As I told her my story, she smiled and nodded her head as if she had more pieces to the puzzle now. She told me she picked them up when she felt the Holy Spirit nudging her to do so. She said that she second-guessed the whole thing as it seemed out of the ordinary but then she listened to His prompting. As I smiled, she explained how she has learned over time to trust and listen to the Holy Spirit when He nudges her to do something like this. It was a wonderful visit and my heart felt lighter from this time with my friend and her thoughtfulness.

Then, just because He could, Jesus had another surprise for me. The next night, I was laying on the couch, in my pajamas with my hair in a messy bun (that's a generous description- the bun looked more like a small nest created in my hair, by a tiny bird, with a few sprigs flailing on the sides). It was 8:30 pm when the doorbell rang. I had no idea who it could be. I crept up to the door and saw that whoever it was had already left. I opened the door and saw a white paper bag with my name on it. I was beyond intrigued at this point. I opened it to find a note from my cousin back in Nova Scotia and a pair of matching earrings, for my daughter and I. It was an early Mother's Day gift. They were locally made by a local vendor and guess what was inside? Yes, that's right, pressed flowers from our town.

Now I have permanent flowers that won't wither and die, as a constant reminder of His pursuit and the generosity and love of my very dear cousin. I thank God for her sweet and thoughtful heart! My eyes filled with tears of joy as I jokingly spoke to God, telling Him He had made His point. I felt like He was laughing with me!

I sent my cousin a video message expressing my surprise and appreciation and explained how God used her to answer my prayer.

These events were a beautiful act of love and mercy from the creator of the earth, and just for me. Talk about pursuit! It was so much more than I deserved, yet he still did it! I was reminded that He has got me in the palm of His hands. If He cares enough to take care of the sparrows, He surely will take care of me. He is working it all out for my good. Knowing and believing that He is protecting me and has good plans for my life helps me to have faith to know that there is no need to worry about my future. If I follow Him and remain close to Him, He will orchestrate my path, all the while pursuing me with an intimate and flawless love. What an amazing God we love and serve.

I hope as you read this, you are aware that Jesus loves you and He does pursue you! These acts quieted my weary heart with His love, and I am beyond thankful for the vessels that He used to answer my prayer. Be looking for His unique answers to prayer and His pursuit of you. If He can orchestrate these events for me, He can speak to your heart in a way that resonates for you. I am blown away that He cares enough about me to do so, yet it is exactly what my heart needed. It felt so intimate. I also thank God for the people He puts in my life. He uses people in your life to help answer prayers, encouraging us along life's tumultuous road. I do not know what I would do without the wonderful support system I have through my family and friends.

> *If He cares enough to take care of the sparrows, He surely will take care of me. He is working it all out for my good.*

One of the most beautiful aspects of relationships with others is when we feel known, accepted, and loved for who we are. When we get to a place with people where we can be authentic and show the good, the bad, and the ugly, there is a new level of love.

There was one time that I traveled with a best friend to California for a winter vacation. We attended a church while we were there. Now, I grew up in a Baptist denomination that was quite reserved. I had some nervousness regarding the pentecostal atmosphere at this church and wasn't sure what to expect, but I also wanted to grow and stretch and meet Jesus in ways I had never before. She explained to me that when the Holy Spirit moved and spoke, it would always be edifying to the body of Christ. This gave my heart peace and I was anticipating revelation during this trip. I asked God to speak to me; very obviously. I wanted it to be like nothing I'd ever experienced before. I wanted the experience to be bold; so obvious that there was no way I could logically reason out that it was anything but the Holy Spirit working.

We got to the church and attended some of the worship services! It was absolutely AMAZING! I was still healing from wounds of my dark season; a time when my pursuit of being wanted to take the forefront. My heart was not aligned with Jesus and neither were my actions.

After, we met up with a group of girls who attended the church; wonderful ladies but complete strangers to us. It was just supposed to be us all hanging out at the coffee shop and getting to know each other. I had literally been with these girls for a few minutes, not knowing them at all. They also knew nothing of me.

Across the table, sat a beautiful, brown-eyed girl named Hannah in her early twenties. In Hebrew, Hannah means favour or grace and it was a name that suited her well. She was very graceful. She had chestnut brown curly hair and a gentle demeanor. The conversation ebbed and flowed until somehow our eyes met and she smiled at me and began prophesying over me.... It was elegant, beautiful, and gentle. It was God-honouring, respectful, and encouraging to my heart. Most of all, it was astonishing because the things she told me, things that the Father told her to say to me, were things she could NEVER have known. Some things no one had ever known because they had never been spoken out loud, but only in my heart. They addressed the darkest longing and hurts, the lies that took away my hope, and the fear that remained in my heart and soul about the future. They shed a beautiful and life-giving hope to every aspect of my story.

The rest of the girls listened, quietly, almost in a state of worship of God as His truths were spoken over my life. Two of the girls wrote down the things Hannah said to me so I could have them later on. Truly the most beautiful gift! I still have them to this day on my hope board. Here are some of the things Hannah told me that my father wanted me to know:

*He gave me a heart of tenderness,*
*He will give me bravery rather than anxiety.*
*He is proud of me.*
*It is strategic that he placed me with children. I will raise people who know who they are.*
*He is restoring dreams in my heart.*
*He is breathing on those places.*
*He hears my prayers for family. It's safe to hope.*

*He will give me bravery and courage.*
*You're so worth it!*
*I don't have you on a timeline.*
*Let yourself be held by me*
*You're a really good friend*
*You're not my second choice*
*Let me pursue you and heal you.*

You are seen by God, made to be loved, made for miracles, free to fly high, lovely, passionate for Jesus, creative, made with a song, carrier of joy, beautiful and wholehearted.

There was no judgment; no sense of confusion. There was only gentleness, hope, peace, and agreement. It was this beautiful moment that renewed my soul, met longings in my heart in a way nothing else ever could. As I listened to her words, all I could do was cry. I was overwhelmed by all the truths that were spoken, the deepest parts of me that were exposed but in a gracious and empowering way. I remember an overwhelming peace and agreement as she listed all of these things. Every time I thought that was it, she said something else that hit me even deeper. It was unbelievable.

I've never spoken to Hannah again but God used her to encourage me and change my outlook on my relationship with Him forever. I'm so grateful for that. God not only uses your friends and family to minister to your heart, He can use complete strangers!

Now, how could a person not feel known, loved, and seen by their Maker after that? We cried together with joy. I was truly astonished. I had never felt so known and the knowledge that she could speak to my circumstances could only have been given to her by God. Some I had never articulated to anyone in my life. Even more ridiculous, this was on February 15, 2018. On May 8 of 2018, I got the call to adopt my sweet daughter!

Back in 2018, certain things Hannah said had strongly stuck a cord with me. It's what my soul was longing for; significance, redemption, and worth. Now, as I go back to read the things she said to me, I resonate with other statements that were said and they are being prophesied to me in this season through that moment. One that has remained true is that God doesn't have me on a timeline. I need to just let Him hold me... isn't that what a little bird would do when he finally found His safe haven and nourishment? Stay there a little longer, and enjoy the comfort and safety of the provision. That's what I want to do too.

Whenever I feel lonely, scared, unworthy, or unseen, I go back to my encounters with Jesus. I have had many significant moments but this one tops them all for sure. Is there anything more intimate than our Saviour knowing us on this level? Beyond knowing us, pursuing us, and fighting for our favour and joy. I can't imagine anything that can even come close to comparing to this beautiful intimacy that God has given me. I want to remain in Him so that I can experience it more and more.

I need to just let Him hold me
isn't that what a little bird would
do when he finally found His safe
haven and nourishment?

_____

# Exchanging Striving for a Sustaining Perspective

*A heart at peace gives life to the body, but envy rots the bones.*
*– Proverbs 14:30*

A few summers ago, I was visiting my family in Nova Scotia. It was my first summer home with my daughter, who was four at the time. I was so excited for her to experience all of the family traditions and adventures we enjoyed that felt like a special part of my childhood. I remember making an extensive list of all the places I wanted to take her on our summer vacation, and my mom gently laughed as
I listed them off. She reminded me that I didn't have to get it all done this summer and we'd have the rest of our lives to enjoy those places and traditions together. She was right! I needed to slow down, stop planning, and just enjoy being together.

We took her to a local farm and greenhouse to go strawberry picking for the first time ever. Our family loves fresh strawberries, especially in my mother's chocolate strawberry shortcake. It's honestly so delicious and has become one of my favourite summer desserts. I could already anticipate the scrumptious dessert as we drove slowly through the parking lot, following the instructions of the parking attendants to our place in the strawberry fields.

As we drove in, I explained to her why I was so excited and that it was totally fine, even encouraged, to sample a few berries while we were picking; it's the best part. We unloaded our boxes and were directed to our row. As I picked the strawberries, we marveled at how red, big, and juicy they were, eating plenty as we picked. She had strawberry juice running down her face. The sun was shining, it was a beautiful day, and I was fulfilling one of the dreams I wanted to experience with her back in my hometown.

As we kept picking, I started looking around at the other rows of strawberry plants. Eventually, my eyes caught the glistening sheen of a ripe, red berry in a row over. At first I just noticed them and commented on how good they looked. We admired them from our row until I could no longer resist them. I finally jumped over the row to pick the berries. They looked so irresistible and I wasn't disrupting anybody by doing so. I only planned to grab the few big berries and return to where I belonged.

When I got there, I assured my mother that this row did have better berries. I picked one and held it up to show her. I kept seeing bigger, better berries and picking them. I am pretty sure I jumped over a few rows here and there, delightfully picking all the choice berries. I was convinced my choice to move rows was making my boxes have the best quality. All seemed well.

Then I noticed some bigger berries further ahead in my previous row and jumped a few rows back to get to those. Once I got back in my row, I was substantially further ahead than my mother and my daughter. I looked back at them to see how they were doing and saw that I had missed some exquisite berries in my original section before I started hopping all over the place. I was momentarily confused as I was pretty sure I had scoped out that section. However, from further down the line, and a new vantage point, I could see all the beautiful berries that I had passed, that were specifically designated for me. I missed them all because of my admiration for berries in the other rows.

I scurried back to my daughter and Mom to get those berries and momentarily thought about how chaotic I must have looked jumping around here, there, and everywhere; all in search of the best berries. Now I was ending back up where I started, where I was directed to be. As I walked back to my family and began picking the berries I had missed, I laughed at my own silliness. Here I was jumping all over the place thinking that my actions were making my box better and more desirable. Now I was back in the same place, picking the berries that were literally in front of me. I missed them because I was so hung up on what I saw in another row. I chuckled as I shared my thoughts with my mother, explaining that this outing was teaching me a valuable life lesson, in the form of a wonderful metaphor for how we walk through life.

I felt like God used this moment as a humorous, yet gentle reminder to be present. Stop being so focused on the good things you see in other rows or in others' lives. Don't be envious of something that someone else has, whether that is a material thing or a situation. It's not for you; maybe not right now, maybe not at all. If that's where your eyes are pointed, you'll miss what is right in front of you, just as I had missed the prime berries that were in front of me. Stop looking so far ahead to what looks so appealing but is currently out of reach, that you miss the choice things that are right in front of you. Perspective is key!

> *Stop looking so far ahead to what looks so appealing but is currently out of reach, that you miss the choice things that are right in front of you. Perspective is key!*

When you are ahead in life and look back with a different perspective, you'll be able to see things you possibly couldn't see while you were there. Hidden gems; blessings that God has tucked away for you in the place that you are. Unfortunately, unlike my escapades in the strawberry patch, we don't always have the opportunity to go back. So it's essential that we savour where we are and what God has for us in our current season.

Sometimes I am convicted that I have missed out on experiencing joy with Jesus, or the people He has blessed me with in my current season of life, because I've been too focused on something I want that I saw in someone else's life or fantasizing about the future. I have all these grand plans of traveling the world with my daughter and making wonderful memories. They are great plans, but it's so important that I stay present and enjoy the bike rides, Disney movies, mind-boggling questions, and conversations that blow my mind, making me laugh or cry. I need to bask in her exuberant laughter and sweet cuddles that make up so much of our family dynamic right now. There are blessings in those things that may not seem obvious at the time, but I know I will look back and cherish and miss them in the future.

My daughter is growing up so quickly and I've already seen seasons of my parenting journey pass and change rapidly as she grows up. I want to be present in every moment; not waste any time comparing my life to someone else's journey. I'm trying to trust Jesus with the future.

Stay focused in your "lane" of blessings, responsibilities, callings, and opportunities for growth- the things that God has put in your life right now. He has you there for a purpose and there will be fruit that will come out of this season. The things that you see in other people's lives may not be bad things, they may be desirable and good things for you, but that's not where God has you right now. So, be present!

> *Stay focused in your "lane" of blessings, responsibilities, callings, and opportunities for growth- the things that God has put in your life right now. He has you there for a purpose and there will be fruit that will come out of this season.*

Maybe you are in a beautiful season and experiencing much joy and hope, enjoy that place! Be present with Jesus and those in your life at that time. Maybe you are making it through, day by day, be encouraged; God will cause useful and beautiful things to come out of this season for you; things that will mold your character, making you stronger and surely drawing you closer to Him. Though sorrow may last for the night, His joy comes in the morning (Psalm 30:5). I promise, joy is coming!

As hard as it seems, press through, be present in your season and there will be beauty to take out of this journey. Whatever situation you find yourself in, know that God has you there for a purpose. With His plans and His perfect timing, it is beautiful or is becoming a marvelous thing. So enjoy what He has for you now, because there is good in it.

Somebody else's "lane" has things that are good for them, but maybe you aren't ready for that yet. Maybe God has something completely different for you that you never anticipated, and that will be even better for you... all in God's perfect timing. Trust the "lane" He's got you in! Don't miss out on the loveliness around you by wishing you had what was in someone's life. Find the beauty in the mundane of life and ask Jesus for joy in the here and now.

After decades of searching for contentment, it came from a surprising source: the stillness and the silence. Contentment came when I stopped; stopped trying, stopped striving. It came when I just was still, listening for the voice of my Saviour. Now, when I start to feel restless, it's my cue to slow down and find myself in Him again.

Maybe God has something completely different for you that you never anticipated, and that will be even better for you... all in God's perfect timing.

# Exchanging Grumbling for Sustaining Gratitude

*It is good to praise the LORD and make music to your name, O Most High, proclaiming Your love in the morning and Your faithfulness at night.*

*- Psalm 92:1-2*

The year after I adopted my daughter was a wonderful whirlwind of blessing, joy, and at times, exhausting change. I went from a single working woman to a full-time, single mother of an active and adjusting toddler. It was a glorious time filled with so much joy, redemption, and hope for the future. For me, it was one of the first, bigger desires of my heart that was actually coming true. So many years of waiting made this time exceptionally special for my family. I wouldn't change it for the world, but when I look back, it is evident that this sudden change had a huge impact on my life.

I took nine months to be at home with her and had given less than three weeks' notice before leaving my job the previous May. Thankfully, we got to spend an extended amount of time back in Nova Scotia with my family, where my daughter got to connect and attach to her cousins, aunts, uncles, grandparents, and great-grandparents. Our stay in Nova Scotia included Christmas vacation with the family. It was a surreal experience of our first Christmas together and I will cherish those memories forever. Sadly, right after New Year's, I came down with a sickness that depleted my body to a state I had never experienced before.

I won't go into the gory details, but I'll give you a summary- two hospital visits for dehydration, we moved a mattress into the bathroom for days so I didn't have too far to go, fevers, and actual fear of what was going to happen. To top it all off, my throat was completely raw. I don't mean sore or even some version of strep throat- I mean raw. I had no voice, every swallow was extremely painful. I had never experienced so much pain for such a long time. We had to rebook our flights back home because I was too sick to leave Nova Scotia to return to Grande Prairie and take care of my daughter on my own.

The sickness lasted over a month and the doctors didn't know what to tell me; they gave me two possibilities, both which would require a longer period of recovery time. It was like the stomach flu with strep throat on steroids. Little did I know at the time, it would take months for me to heal and years for my voice and throat to heal. It's been four years now and my voice is still extremely fragile when I overuse it.

We finally returned home less than a week before I started back to work after my nine-month leave. My little girl had to begin attending a day home and our whole sense of normalcy would be uprooted again just as we had finally found our groove. I still was not feeling well. So, as you can imagine, I was tired and stressed, and just low in general. I started back to work still sick, struggling to speak with a weak voice.

It seems like when it rains, it pours. On my first day back to work, with a frigid temperature of -45 degrees celsius, my power steering stopped working in my car. I had to strong-arm it to the dealership and I didn't know it at the time, but it would take weeks to get it serviced. I was given a loaner car from the dealership to use and was less than confident in its ability to function in our wild winters in the northwest, as it was a small car with no winter tires. This obviously added to my stress.

Coming back to one's classroom halfway through the year is just awful. The kids don't see you as their teacher; understandably, I wasn't. The lady who was hired for my leave was their teacher. Therefore, I was not met with eager and excited faces like I was used to but instead with tearful eyes that missed someone who had become their safe place.

It was a hard transition for all of us. By the end of the first week, my voice was completely gone again and there was no way I could teach without some sort of medicinal intervention. I was hoping for a quick fix with medicine but my doctor informed me that it was a viral infection and it had to run its course. She told me I needed to take a week off of work and talk as little as possible. I tried to explain that I couldn't as I had just gone back to work but she was firm in her prescribed advice: no medicine, just rest. So, five weeks after starting with this ridiculous flu, I was still sick and heading home on sick leave.

My head swirled with the thoughts of the poor impression that I was creating for my new students' parents and what other staff members might think or say about my absences. I was exhausted from the transition and upset with how things were unfolding. I was brought to the reality that I couldn't control this in my life and had to let go of my plans. But I also was questioning God as to why he was letting things unfold as they did. Why did I come back for just one week, just to leave again? Now the kids would have a different sub for the following week.

After a long day at work, and several hours working on sub plans that skimmed the surface of planning for my absences the following week, my daughter and I climbed in the car to quickly get some medicinal supplies and then go home. A sweet colleague had offered us the rest of her soup that she brought to a staff social, which took place at lunch. I excitedly accepted this offer. It meant supper was already made. What a blessing that was with my current physical and emotional state. So, the soup was packed in a box, inside a slow cooker, and placed in the trunk of the rental car.

Now this is where I need to explain winter conditions in Grande Prairie, Alberta. The winter weather is bipolar in its temperatures and because of this, road maintenance can be rather poor; the streets don't get plowed as often as they need to be. The city does the best it can but it really seems to be the wild, wild west in the winter months. People still drive to where they need to go, which packs the snow down into the roads. This creates a white canvas with no lines or divisions that one would be used to seeing.

During this particular week, there was an average of -35 degrees and the snow had gotten packed down into the roads that we drove home. The cars clunked along the streets, barely functioning in the dead of winter. The tire tracks in the road create clearly indented lines packed down the snow, making grooves that your wheels have no choice but to follow. When you drive through intersections and hit these intersecting grooves at a perpendicular angle, you experience a catastrophic bump as your car's shocks ache from the abrupt and unforeseen changes in the road.

So, as we headed to the drug store to get some throat lozenges and other things to prepare for my week of silence, my car hit the perpendicular groove in the road. I heard an awful sound of the crockpot being jostled in the trunk. I shuttered and asked myself, will the box contain the mess? Is it going to be everywhere? In a rental car no less! We were only about thirty seconds from the drugstore but my heart pounded as I drove those thirty seconds wondering what the state of the trunk of this rental car was.

I opened the trunk to reveal a heavy smattering of chicken and chili soup, in a creamy, ranch base, spread all over the trunk. It was a disaster that had meshed itself into the upholstery of the trunk. I bolted inside the store to buy some Lysol wipes, or anything to clean up the mess, but forgot that at -35, things pretty much freeze instantly. By the time I got back out to the car, the soup was frozen to the lining of the trunk. This was going to be a much more painful endeavour to clean than I anticipated, so I thought I might as well go home, eat supper, get my daughter to bed, and then come back to tackle it. So, that's exactly what I did.

All the while, I was angered by my current circumstances:

strict orders from my doctor not to speak for a week; making sub plans for a job that I just returned to and agonizing about how that looked to others; and using a rental car because mine wasn't working, which I just covered in frozen soup because we live in the coldest place on earth (which literally was announced that week on Facebook). The soup was the last straw and I was emotionally spent.

A few hours later, with scalding, soapy water and a cloth, I faced the trunk in the dark, wintery night. The cold air was accentuated by the steamy, hot water, and with each dip in the bucket, my hands were aching as I scrubbed and picked up chunks of frozen soup. With each moment, I was getting increasingly infuriated.

I was overwhelmed with frustration and anxiety and sank into a vat of self-pity replaying all the terrible things happening in my week.

I was about to start crying in my pathetic misery when the Holy Spirit gently nudged at my heart and encouraged me to count my blessings: Breathe. Just stop and take a breath. There is still so much to be thankful for. Think about those things. It was a gentle but direct reminder. It hit me hard enough that even with my lack of voice, I started listing the things I was thankful for- out loud in my driveway; realizing this might look straight-up crazy to my neighbours. Mind you, it was -35! No one else would be hanging around outside at this ridiculous temperature!

I started with a basic list: having food to eat, a roof over our heads, and a bed to sleep in. My heart was moved as I spoke out each thing I was thankful for. I internally thought of the possibilities of what it could look like instead...

*I have a warm house that I could go back into after I cleaned this mess up.* There were people on the street tonight who would feel this harsh cold all night. At these temperatures, death is actually a possibility for those who are homeless.

*I still have a car, even if it is a loaner and I didn't have to pay for it while my car was getting fixed.* Imagine if I had to rent a car for all of those days, the extra financial stress it could have caused me. Worse yet, the people that don't have cars and have to take buses or walk. My problem with my car was only temporary, and the blessing of a vehicle in these conditions was not something to be taken lightly.

*I have a job where I could take a week off after being gone for nine months without a financial penalty.* Many people have jobs where taking five days off would be impossible or have many ramifications for their paycheque and employment. During this thought process, I realized, if I hadn't started back to work, I would still be receiving Employment Insurance, which is substantially less than my salary which I was now going to be paid even during this absence, plus my benefits were being covered by my employer again and not out of my own pocket. I realized the timing was actually in my favour financially even though I had earlier questioned God about the timing.

*I have a beautiful, joy-filled daughter whom I love to a depth I didn't know was possible.* A little girl who was transitioning so well to monumental changes in her life over the last nine months. I had found a wonderful day home that was loving my child in my absence and provided great peace to this part *of the transition. The alternative could have been that she could have not adjusted so well or I could have been worried about her childcare situation.*

These were the big-ticket items that humbled me. As the list went on, I was overwhelmed by my petty and self-centered mindset. Sure, the events of the week and night were frustrating but certainly not earth-shattering. With each exclamation of thankfulness, I felt a little bitterness, anger, and self-pity descend. I could actually laugh at the situation, knowing it would be a humorous story in the future. Proverbs 17:22 says, *"A cheerful heart is good medicine, but a crushed spirit dries up the bones"* (NRSV). A cheerful heart can also come from a thankful heart. It is healing! When I was focused on all the disappointments, I was crushed and defeated. When I focused on the blessings, I became more joy-filled in the midst of a challenging circumstance.

> *When I was focused on all the disappointments, I was crushed and defeated. When I focused on the blessings, I became more joy-filled in the midst of a challenging circumstance.*

As I continued to talk to God in my driveway that night, my heart went from an anxiety-ridden state to a restful place where I found stillness in Him and a little sense of humour too. The biggest change was that I went from being ungrateful to thankful for the things I had in my life; knowing the challenges I faced were temporary. The things that really mattered from a kingdom perspective were solid and that's where I needed to thank my gracious heavenly Father for blessing us!

Hebrew 12:28-29 states, *"Therefore, since we are receiving a kingdom that cannot be shaken, let us be thankful, and so worship God acceptably with reverence and awe, for our 'God is a consuming fire'."* The kingdom that cannot be shaken is an eternal one. When we keep that focus, the trials and challenges become easier to look past because our gaze is focused on eternity with our Saviour; not these momentary afflictions.

Our heavenly Father has got us under His wing and He has a plan, even when we don't understand it or can't see it. Trusting Him and resting in that knowledge is such a better way to go through life than trying to figure it out ourselves. I'm reminded of the verses in Matthew 6:25-35 that say:

> *Therefore I tell you, do not worry about your life, what you will eat or drink; or about your body, what you will wear. Is not life more than food, and the body more than clothes? Look at the birds of the air; they do not sow or reap or store away in barns, and yet your heavenly Father feeds them. Are you not much more valuable than they? Can any one of you by worrying add a single hour to your life? And why do you worry about clothes? See how the flowers of the field grow. They do not labor or spin. Yet I tell you that not even Solomon in all his splendor was dressed like one of these. If that is how God clothes the grass of the field, which is here today and tomorrow is thrown into the fire, will He not much more clothe you—you of little faith? So do not worry, saying, 'What shall we eat?' or 'What shall we drink?' or 'What shall we wear?' For the pagans run after all these things, and your heavenly Father knows that you need them. But seek first His kingdom and His righteousness, and all these things will be*

*given to you as well. Therefore do not worry about tomorrow, for tomorrow will worry about itself. Each day has enough trouble of its own."*

If God could take care of the ravens and magpies up in Northern Alberta at minus a billion degrees and design a world where the rebirth of the flowers comes every spring after facing the cruelty of winter, He can and will most certainly take care of us. In many ways, He is taking care of us and meeting needs we didn't even realize we had.

What had been so upsetting to me turned out to be another blessing. I used the week at home to organize my house to an extent it had never been. I spent my days talking and listening to God. I do not think listening has ever been a great strength of mine. So at first, I fought it. Then I decided to embrace it. In instances where I would normally be direct and active, my lack of ability to speak created a passive nature, birthing an entirely new perspective in my mind and heart. I began hearing the words of worship music more distinctly because I was listening in a way I had never done before. I was listening to my daughter's requests and questions and carefully choosing my words to respond back. It caused me to talk less, listen more, and engage with God in a new way. I found myself resting in His stillness and peace more than I ever did before because I was never really forced to stop talking and listen.

I decided that the next time I was met with a situation similar to those discouraging times, I would remember to breathe and take a moment to catch the kingdom perspective that would allow me to deal with the struggle while continuing to be joy-filled. He has provided for me these last thirty years and He will continue to do so!

Even this major inconvenience was transformed into a lasting blessing in my relationship with Christ. There are often times in worship when He will tell me to just be still; not to sing but just to listen. My worship takes on a different stance; one with a different sense of awe. I love the dynamic it has allowed me to enter into within this form of worship. It has become a distinct experience where the words of Romans 8:28 ring true: *"And we know that for those who love God all things work together for good, for those who are called according to His purpose"* (ESV). He knows what I need before I'm even aware of it.

I hope that next time you are in a situation where you feel overwhelmed and angry, you can remember this story and find the nuggets of encouragement that your heart needs. Thank Jesus for the promise of His presence and provision in our lives. This is a guaranteed method to shift grumbling to gratitude. May we trust in Him and find rest in those promises that cover the many facets of our lives. *"The Lord is my strength and my shield; in Him my heart trusts, and I am helped; my heart exults, and with my song I give thanks to Him"* (Psalm 28:7, ESV).

Breathe. Just stop and take a breath. There is still so much to be thankful for. Think about those things.

# Exchanging Sorrow For Sustaining Joy

*Weeping may stay for the night, but rejoicing comes in the morning.*

*- Psalm 30:5b*

During the pandemic, I experienced another season of sorrow. One that was a more subtle, numbing, and disillusioning season that impacted my hope. One did not need to look very far to see hardship, and with it, an understandably broken spirit. Of course, everyone's stories are unique and consist of their own particular trials, but my heart gravitated to the loss and ache that so many people in my life had experienced during that time.

How does the human heart even handle such loss? At times, I was overwhelmed just imagining the pain that people in my life had experienced: the death of a loved one through an overdose, my brother's diagnosis of cancer, two of my friends struggling through the separation and divorce of their families, the mental health crisis due to the pandemic itself, the perpetual weariness of those unfulfilled longings in my life, and an abundance of fear so prevalent in the world at that time. Countless stories left me feeling the ache- for something different than the pain we too often experience in this world. No wonder people feel weary. Just living through the pandemic created stress, but when you add in additional hardships, it tends to leave a heart feeling depleted.

One summer night, my mother and I sat out under the stars in a canoe, and I expressed how my heart ached for all the sadness that people had gone through or were currently battling. It just seemed unfair and, frankly, just too much. We talked about why we longed for heaven; how all of the sin, pain and relational wounds would not be present in heaven. It calmed my soul. In a moment of

> *If we didn't ache from a place of brokenness, we wouldn't long for perfection.*

reflection, I shared with my mom, "If we didn't ache from a place of brokenness, we wouldn't long for perfection." This statement has stayed with me and is one that steadies my soul when I feel the overwhelming weight of this world's brokenness. Every time I hear of another betrayal, heartache, or hardship, I quote that line to myself. I think we have to look for the beauty within the chaos. God can use difficult circumstances to our benefit- drawing us closer to Him or healing wounds in our souls. If we don't intentionally look for His hand in our circumstances (not that He created those circumstances, but that He is with us through them), it is hard to live with a joyful spirit. And that is what we are called to do. We cannot stay weary and hopeless from the ache; we have to find hope and joy within the ache. For me, the joy set before us is heaven.

C.S. Lewis stated, *"If I find in myself desires which nothing in this world can satisfy, the most probable explanation is that I was made for another world."*[11] I believe this wholeheartedly. We were not made for this world; the way it operates is broken by sin. We were made for a world without sin. It takes a toll on our hearts. One day, we will experience a world without sin, and I for one look forward to that day.

Hebrews 12:2 explains that Jesus endured the cross, for the sake of the joy set before Him. This statement blows my mind. It shows me how marred my perspective on life and faith really is. We are called to follow Jesus' example. What Jesus was called to experience was a horrific burden. I can't imagine the pain He endured during the crucifixion. He did it for the joy which was to come, which is described as sitting at the right hand of God: to be and to reign with Him. Don't we have the same thing to look forward to as followers of Christ? This is how we find our joy and along with that, our hope for the future.

Just like a mother endures the discomfort and pain of carrying a child for nine months because she knows that the joy that will come from the birth of that baby is far better than any pain she is currently experiencing, so it is with our waiting. We endure parts of this life, aching to experience the beauty of Heaven and the renewal it will provide for us. We know that our endurance will be well-worth the sweet reward that we

> *Whatever we experience here on this earth will seem so insignificant when we experience the splendor and majesty of our Lord and our new heavenly home.*

---

11. Lewis, C F M. 1977. Mere Christianity. Glasgow: Fount Paperbacks.

can expect in the Heavenly realms in the presence of our glorious King! Whatever we experience here on this earth will seem so insignificant when we experience the splendor and majesty of our Lord and our new heavenly home.

When I am in the midst of my own battle or even overwhelmed when hearing about the heartache of another, I have to remind myself, *If I didn't ache from the way this world is, what would drive me to long for heaven?* To me, it is a similar concept to the idea of *without suffering, there'd be no compassion.*[12] It takes one journey to be able to appreciate the other. While we are here on earth, we need to face these trials with a joyful faith. Not from joy that we can muster up ourselves- goodness no! I am so thankful we are not left on our own. We can have steady faith, peace, and joy when resting in the knowledge that Jesus is fighting for us in these battles.

I still am learning to live with this mindset as my dominant way of processing life's events.. I have my moments, but in the future I'd love to have longer and sustained periods of time where I live with the peace and joy of a heavenly perspective. We will get through the trials of this earth and in comparison, they are truly momentary afflictions compared to the joy that awaits us in heaven. 2 Corinthians 4:17-18 says, *"For our light and momentary affliction is producing for us an eternal weight of glory that is far beyond comparison. So we fix our eyes not on what is seen, but on what is unseen. For what is seen is temporary, but what is unseen is eternal."* What a sweet promise! And what a heart check. Are we focused on the temporary or are we focused on the eternal?

I am in no way meaning to diminish what you are going through. That is not my goal at all. I am just hoping to give you a nugget of

---

12. Sparks, Nicholas. 2004. Walk to Remember. Bt Bound.

encouragement if your heart is in a place to receive that. Perhaps you are currently going through something unbearable. I am so sorry that you are and I hope things get lighter soon, my friend. However, this is the truth and current conviction that I feel Jesus whispering to my heart because we need to have something to fix our eyes on. When you are in the middle of a trial or something that makes your soul ache, try to remember that without the aching in this world, you would not long for the perfection of heaven. If you have a personal relationship with Jesus, this is a truth that you stand firm in. Perfection is coming! A time without pain, tears, or brokenness is coming. So hold on! Don't give up! It'll all be worth it!

We can have steady faith,
peace, and joy when resting in
the knowledge that Jesus is
fighting for us in these battles.

# Exchanging Insufficiency for Sustaining Abundance

*But those who hope in the Lord will renew their strength. They will soar on wings like eagles; they will run and not grow weary, they will walk and not be faint.*

*– Isaiah 40:31*

What am I doing? I can't write a book on being sustained by God. I'm currently failing at parenting; certainly not exemplifying His fruit in my reactions at all. I am not in any place to be a spokesperson for this.

This was my thought as I drove to church one Sunday morning. I was feeling worn out and frantic in trying to accomplish all my responsibilities and had just seen my human nature prove itself in several interactions with my daughter that morning. I was in that place where I could feel the enticing but deceptive pull of my heart to just harden and stop trying and believing the lie that it's just too hard.

Jesus immediately countered my thoughts with a humbling statement: Wouldn't it actually make you the perfect candidate to write the book? When you see a change, you will know it's Me within you and has nothing to do with your own will or power. Isn't that the basic truth of Me sustaining you?

Well.... yeah.... I guess you're right. I answered with a renewed perspective and a smirk at the banter. That's my Jesus; always so gracious. He had an excellent point, and we often have these types of conversations with a simple sentence here and there and then we continue with our day.

To give further context to my emotions, I had found that weekend extremely trying with my daughter. To be honest, she wasn't even being that difficult. I was just burned out and had zero patience. Saturday morning, I drew myself a bath and relaxed while I prayed to be gracious and loving with her. I felt at peace again and refreshed in a sense, and was hopeful for the change that I would see in myself being filled by the Spirit. Literally, less than one hour later, I lost control of my temper over a minor annoyance and saw the beast of anger rise within me again. I felt like such a failure. What happened? How do I go from this peaceful place with a focus on Spirit-filled reactions to a rapid escalation of sinful impulses to our irritations? It's because it doesn't take much to get our hearts and minds off track; a simple thought can lead to choosing to believe a lie, which can lead us to a spiral of life-draining thinking. Then it is so easy to lose perspective and then step outside that unbroken connection with the Spirit.

This was now the next morning as I sat in church, trying to get out of this mental funk of failure. I have this little game I play at church during the worship part of the service where I try to guess what song is coming next based on the intro. I don't know if anyone else does this, I'll blame it on my musician's brain. Well, that particular morning I heard the first notes and there was no game, there was sweet relief. I knew one of my favourite songs was coming, a song that resounded with a needed personal truth. The worship team started singing and I wept as I tried to sing along. I eventually gave up trying to sing through my tears and just let the lyrics echo in my heart.

> *Lord I come, I confess, bowing here, I find my rest*
> *Without You, I fall apart, You're the one that guides my heart*
> *Lord, I need You, oh, I need You, Every hour, I need You*
> *My one defense, my righteousness, Oh God, how I need You*
> *Where sin runs deep, Your grace is more; Where grace*
> *is found is where You are. Where You are, Lord, I am free,*
> *Holiness is Christ in me.*
> *So teach my song to rise to You When temptation*
> *comes my way When I cannot stand, I'll fall on You, Jesus,*
> *You're my hope and stay.*[13]

I had never identified with this song so much, particularly related to my parenting journey. These lyrics are just laced with that idea of abiding in Him; His provision and character are my defense, my righteousness. His holiness and His grace are what I need when my sinful nature rises within and tries to take over again. I prayed that God would soften my heart and break me gently so I would come right back to Him, in humility, and receive His grace and rest.

---

13. Maher, Matt. 2013. Lord I Need You.

I felt Him telling me to go pray with someone after the service, so I did. That sweet lady to whom I explained my struggle was so encouraging, explaining that she understood and had also felt all of those same emotions and trials in her own parenting journey. It felt so comforting to not be alone in that. She prayed a beautiful request to God for my daughter and I and our journey together; that He would bless us and we would both be able to see His hand throughout our lives when we look back. She also prayed for wisdom for me in my parenting journey. My heart felt refreshed, relieved, and a little softer.

I had two other moments in the day where I could feel myself getting annoyed and was able to pray in the moment and allow the Holy Spirit to speak to my daughter through me. It was in a loving way and a way she responded to. I smiled as I knew my prayer had been answered. I feel like whatever was going on in my mind and thoughts over those days, my focus wasn't on an unbroken connection with Jesus, and it was evident to see my struggle through ungodly reactions. Once I took that time, was broken, confessed, and sought His healing and guidance, I could see a longer-lasting difference. Now, this is just one example of a way that parenting grows and challenges us. I'm sure if you're a parent, you have your own memories that flood back to moments when you needed this same intervention.

Parenting is the hardest, yet most rewarding thing I have ever done. I've never felt such investment in another human than my own child. It amazes me how you can love a person so incredibly much and also feel so frustrated by them at the same time. Can I get an amen? It's a paradoxical anomaly that bends the mind but transforms the heart as we walk through the experience. It is such a beautiful, yet exhausting opportunity we have. I am constantly feeling insufficient in my role as a parent. I feel insufficient because I am human and make mistakes; I get too angry, lack patience, and sometimes have expectations that are too high. Yet, I also struggle with the concept of maintaining higher expectations so that she will meet them. You parents know what I'm talking about, right? If you're not a parent, I am sure you can find another role or relationship where you can see similar expectations and interactions occurring.

My feelings of insufficiency in my journey were deeply felt as I chose to adopt my daughter on my own. In essence, I chose to be a single parent. I felt called to do it and God opened up the doors. It was and remains abundantly clear that this was His plan and He reinforces that conviction continually in my life. I have been affirmed in so many ways that adopting my daughter was a gift from God as well as a mission field for me. I also hope that it will be just as evident to her and others that I am a gift to her in her own personal journey. We were meant to be together and God continues to bless our family. I have had so many people step alongside me to support and surround us with love as we navigate this path. He is so good!

Even in the midst of the confirmations, there are aspects of parenting that I didn't realize how tough they could be when there is only one parent. You don't get a break! You're on 100% of the time and you end up doing all the things by yourself that were made for two people to be able to accomplish together. There are moments when I feel the pressure and wish there was someone else to pass the baton to on those occasions when I am just done. When I am exhausted or distracted by other life circumstances, I have less in my tank to give to my daughter. I'm so incredibly thankful for the people in our lives that support us and I want to emphasize my gratitude. Still, at the end of the day, I am a single parent.

All this to say, I have an entire extra set of lies that Satan throws at me when I feel weak. Lies that question my motives for adopting. Lies that belittle my intelligence as a single parent. Lies that cast fears into my future with my daughter wondering how it will unfold. Lies that I am and will always be alone in parenting and life, and because of that, I hear the lie that I am "less than" in the eyes of others. They are easy to believe because I hear them often. I have to be careful to combat these lies with the truth quickly or else my whole spirit can descend into darkness and hopelessness. Have you ever experienced these types of spirals? Do you know how to combat those lies when they creep into your mind?

> *When we join forces with the Holy Spirit and He provides us with supernatural grace and love, it is transformative and life-giving. I know in my moments of grace, it is not me, it's Jesus living within me.*

It can easily end up being this spiral of shame, frustration, and exhaustion as we try to parent well in our own strength. When we join forces with the Holy Spirit and He provides us with supernatural grace and love, it is transformative and life-giving. I know in my moments of grace, it is not me, it's Jesus living within me.

Part of me thought that when I adopted my daughter four years ago, I would eventually meet someone and she would also inherit a father. It wasn't a necessity but it was certainly a hope. I was expecting that this would happen before she got old enough to ask those questions and long for this relationship too. When she started asking why she didn't have a daddy and why wouldn't I just get married so she could have a father and siblings, it made my heart ache that much more. If only it were that simple. Now it wasn't just my wants and desires, it was hers too. It still is. I notice how she is drawn to male figures; her friends' dads or Uncles who have become so important to her. She craves that male attention and longs for it. It intrigues her since she doesn't have that love of her own yet. I think it is completely natural because that is how God created the family to be. Yet in this broken world, there are so many family units that do not look like God's original intention. Even with that element, I see His hand of grace in those families, where children still thrive, experience Him, and experience the healing and redemption He provides.

I understand her desires and wish with her that she can one day have these things. God reminds me that the story isn't over yet; there is more to be written. Whether that means I will get married or not, I don't know. What I have come to believe is that whatever way my life plays out, God is enough. I take every opportunity I get to remind her of this same truth. She will have to come to understand it on her own, but I want her to see her mother believe it and live it out in her faith journey. He will sustain us and be enough for us even though our family is different from many others. I like to remind her, being different isn't a bad thing!

I know I am not the only one who has a family unit that looks different than they imagined. Maybe you are single through divorce, or maybe your spouse died. Maybe you are still married but your spouse is not available to help with parenting as much as you'd like due to distance or disability. Maybe you never had a spouse to begin with. Whatever the case may be, if you seek Him, He will sustain you!

What I can tell you is this: single parenting has made me run to God continually for wisdom, grace, consolation, forgiveness, and a multitude of other needs. I think because I don't have a spouse, I talk to God more to process things and express concerns. I talk to Him throughout the day or during moments of frustration. If I had a spouse to talk it through with regularly, maybe I wouldn't be talking to God as much as I do. That's a perfect example of God using my particular circumstances to be a blessing in our relationship. Seeking after God in this role in my life has changed things radically. I had to accept that I couldn't do it well within my own strength.

It has become clear to me that God is using this time in my life to mold me and that it has required me to be alone. It's not that I feel called to be alone, I still long for companionship and would love to experience marriage. It just isn't happening right now. So for this season, I am alone. I am learning more and more to be comfortable in my singleness. Instead of being lonely, I pursue finding my companionship in Christ, enjoying other types of relationships, thanking Him for my child who brings me joy and a family unit, and we can't forget those two furry canine companions that are part of our family, bringing us a different type of companionship, along with a sense of security.

I know not all of you are animal lovers and that's fine. You can glaze over this part. However, I am! Gratefulness and joy exude from my daughter and me in our daily interactions with these two pups, Harley and Khalani. They are always happy when we come home, they make us laugh, can sense when something is off, and come take care of us in the only way they know how, by licking our faces off. Lastly, and even better than a child or spouse, they don't talk back... well, for the most part!

When we go for a walk, with my two trusty companions on either side of me, it is one of my greatest sources of providing safety for us. I really enjoy living with them and feel the ability to rest, as I know I am protected when I am with them. You may not need this in your life, but for me, it has become essential. I regularly thank God for creating these furry beasts that we can attach to and make memories with.

I don't know how long this season of singleness will last but I intend to enjoy it and learn from it so that if I ever have a season of companionship through marriage, I will be able to be a healthy and complimentary spouse. God continually shows me more areas where I need His refinement. As exhausting as it can sometimes feel, He is so gentle about it.

The world tells me because I am single, I am less than. I fight against those messages. He tells me that because He is with me and in me, I am more than enough. Not because of who I am in my own strength, but who I am with His power inside of me. The same power that raised Jesus from the dead can live inside of us (Romans 6:10-11). How can we feel insufficient when we have that revelation? He sustains me. He comforts me. He speaks with me. He is my companion. He empowers me.

> *He tells me that because He is with me and in me, I am more than enough. Not because of who I am in my own strength, but who I am with His power inside of me.*

I heard this analogy in a sermon many years ago. It hit me hard and has stuck with me when it comes to knowing my value and identity in Christ:

> The young soldier, a recent recruit and a private, was at the lowest rank in the army. He was part of a large military exercise and he and several of his teammates had just returned from nighttime patrol. It was breakfast time and they had a few minutes to eat before they had to report for the next assignment. They were tired and hungry. As they sat down to eat their breakfast, another soldier came up to their table and asked if he could join them. Before looking up they mumbled agreement, but then one of the privates glanced at the man standing beside them and noticed the rank emblems of a brigadier general and all the young men snapped to nervous attention.
>
> This man was the highest-ranking soldier involved in the exercise and they were the lowest. It turns out that the brigadier general had started his military career in the same trade as the privates so he wanted to chat with them about their experiences. After a pleasant, albeit, short conversation, the privates mentioned that they needed to return to their area to report. The brigadier general told them there was no hurry as the next exercise would not begin until he said so, and he offered to walk with them to their barracks. Being privates, the young men were very conscious of the fact that they needed to be ready to salute all the officers moving about the compound.
>
> Not knowing how they should act when walking with the brigadier general, one private asked him. He replied, "When

*you walk in company with me, you salute no one because
you are seen to be with me and no one here outranks me!"
The young men walked with the brigadier general and all
the many officers snapped to* attention and saluted the
brigadier general as they passed and the young men felt
very special indeed.[14]

I tell you this story because it is a picture of our lives in Christ.
When we accept Christ's finished work on the cross for us, we
enter into a relationship with Him. We no longer live in our own
authority, but we live and act in the authority of the King of Kings
and the Lord of Lords. We no longer need to fear and bow to the
power of sin or the forces of this world because greater is He who is in us than he who is in the world (1 John 4:4). We now walk with the Lord of Glory! I loved this analogy, and it

> *Your value isn't based on what you bring to the table. You are insufficient on our own. With Jesus by your side, your sufficiency flows from His grace and righteousness.*

emphasized the point to me that their personal identity no longer
mattered once they were walking in step with the top-ranking
officer. By walking with him, they took on his rank.

Doesn't Jesus do the same thing for us? When we walk with
Him, our rank no longer matters. Our merit is not based on how
many times we control our tempers over spilled milk or broken
dishes or how many times we fail to do so. Our sufficiency doesn't
come from the applause and appreciation of those who see
aspects of our lives, or the judgment and condemnation from those
same circles when we don't meet their standards. Your value isn't
based on what you bring to the table. You are insufficient on our

---

14. Michels, Stephen. Letter to Julianna Davidson. 2019. "Request for Sermon Analogy." Facebook Messenger, April 19, 2019.

own. With Jesus by your side, your sufficiency flows from His grace and righteousness. You can be confident that He will sustain you in this way, giving you an abundance of energy, wisdom, patience, and grace for those moments when you are lacking some. He also gives you an abundance of forgiveness and redemption when you do completely blow it.

I pray that you take these examples into your own circumstance where you are currently feeling insufficient. Trade in those feelings of insufficiency for abundance and watch God work things out in ways you could have not predicted. Better ways. Life-giving ways!

With Jesus by your side, your
sufficiency flows from His grace
and righteousness.

_____

# Exchanging Anger for Sustaining Grace to Forgive

*But you, O Lord, are a God merciful and gracious, slow to anger and abounding in steadfast love and faithfulness.*

*- Psalm 86:15, ESV*

Growing up, I didn't see myself as an overly angry person. I felt deeply, but it was usually feelings of sadness. It did not manifest itself as anger. However, into adulthood, anger started to rear its ugly head, and it really became prominent when I became a parent. Parenting has a way of humbling you by revealing the flaws that didn't seem so obvious until you are continually put in situations where you see how selfish you actually are. It expedites the process of highlighting aspects of your character that you need

God's grace and transformation. For me, anger was one of them.

I can gratefully say that over the last few years, I have seen His healing touch in this area of my life. I have dealt with some of my baggage that aided me in becoming angry so quickly. I still have moments of anger, but the Lord gives me the strength to handle it in a much more loving and gracious way. I am continually and lovingly challenged by my Heavenly Father to show my daughter as much grace as the Lord has shown me. I am sure I am not the only person who can relate to this feeling.

This is the chapter I have had the hardest time articulating. I believe God has given me the words to speak, so I am sitting down at 11pm to start writing while I can clearly hear Him, even though it feels much too late for writing. I want to talk about those relational wounds and the anger that often comes with them. Pain, followed by anger. It's such a common path we walk in this world. At least, I know I do.

I'm sure you don't have to think too hard before you can remember a time when you have felt angry about something. I'm not saying that anger in itself is wrong, there is such a thing as righteous anger. However, doing things in an angry state doesn't usually bring forth better circumstances in our relationships. James 1:20 reiterates this concept by stating, *"...for the anger of man does not produce the righteousness of God"* (ESV). Handling anger is a challenging task. It becomes a problem when we don't forgive because it holds us back. When we hold onto anger, we are actually sinning as we are not forgiving as Christ told us to; like He has done for us repeatedly. For me, unforgiveness creates distance in our relationship with the Holy Spirit.

Anger is not an emotion we experience in isolation. By this, I mean it is a secondary emotion. When we feel anger, it is because another feeling is fueling it. Possible companions to anger are feelings of rejection, injustice, marginalization, disrespect, vulnerability, neglect, or just plain old hurt.[15] To deal with our anger, it becomes essential for us to identify the other feelings that are fueling our reactions. Usually, they are triggered by something that has happened to us previously. However, we are warned that it is something we should take care of. Ecclesiastes 7:9 tells us, *"Be not quick in your spirit to become angry, for anger lodges in the heart of fools"* (ESV).

We can all remember a time in our lives when we have been wounded by another person because of things done or said. Relationships are things that provide so much joy, yet also create so much pain. They provide us with companionship; someone with whom we can enjoy life, process circumstances, and be known on a deeper level. However, when things hurt us in relationships, it is often because we feel overlooked, unknown, or treated unjustly.

Can you think of a time when someone has hurt you because of those unforgettable words? Or an action towards you that seemed hateful? Or a lack of action, that made you feel unworthy or unwanted? Maybe it's betrayal; maybe it was intentional, maybe it was not. Possibly the person is completely unaware that they have impacted you. That can also hurt in a completely different way. We want to know that we matter to people. When their actions don't show that they care, hurt and unforgiveness can start to creep in.

Every action that I can think of that has caused me pain, I can link back to brokenness; whether it belongs to me or someone

15. "Anger: A Secondary Emotion." n.d. Creducation.net. https://creducation.net/resources/anger_management/anger__a_secondary_emotion.html.

else. There is a wound or a trigger that causes us to respond the way we do. It doesn't make it right, and it doesn't make it fair. God has given me the grace to see that some of the people that have hurt me the most are hurting in their own ways; they are in their own personal trial or struggle. I may not understand it or even know about it but as I've lived, God has shown me often that broken people are at a higher risk of breaking other people.

So what do we do with that knowledge? The damage is still done. The relationship is still tainted or in some cases, severed. I'm not going to dance around this one. Jesus is the only answer. He is the only place where you will find healing. The Holy Spirit is the only one who can give you the grace to forgive when He abides in you. He shows love and forgiveness when your own nature cannot fathom it.

Someone once told me that forgiveness toward a person sometimes is something that happens over and over again. This occurs because you can only forgive to the point of what you understand at the time. Sometimes, at a later date, more understanding comes. Therefore, more hurt comes and more forgiveness is needed. This is where I have seen Jesus lavish His grace within me so that I can have grace for others. Without Him, I am scared to think of where my anger could lead me.

How about you? What are you angry about? Who do you still find hard to think about or feel that raw ache in your heart when they come to your mind? If you don't have anyone that brings you to that place, rejoice! If you do, then go get some healing! God is good and wants to heal you from that pain!

I have recently started going to these counseling sessions called Inner Healing.[16] The premise is that we all have moments and memories from our past that have wounded us. It could be because of the actions of another, or it could be that we believed a lie about ourselves at that moment because of how we perceived the situation to unfold, whether intentional or not. Some of those lies we can still carry around with us.

With the help of a professional and the Holy Spirit, the counselors lead you back to childhood memories or the moment when you first felt pain, which led you to believe a lie. They ask you to go back and relive the moment. They pray and ask Jesus to reveal the truth to you at that moment. In some memories, I've even been led to ask where Jesus was in that moment, and I am able to find Him and His truth for me. It is exhausting and dark at times, but real and raw and allows for deep healing.

The wonderful part is that after you address those lies and hear God's truth for you, you can start to focus on that. I am noticing that certain events or responses do not trigger anger or feelings of shame in me like they used to. It truly feels like a miracle when you see for yourself that you are responding differently. The glory of the situation can only be attributed to God because He is the one that is changing you. For example, in one of my sessions, my focus was on a movie I recently watched that came highly recommended by many people. I found it to be traumatizing and triggering on many levels. When I told my counselor which movie it was, she had read the book, watched the movie, and expressed that it was well done and something she enjoyed. She didn't have the same sentiments toward it at all.

---

16. "Rising above Ministries - Inner Healing." 2022. www.risingabovegp.com. 2022. https://www.risingabovegp.com/InnerHealing1.

At first, this baffled me. I think I was almost offended by it. As we talked, it was evident that my personal experiences made this movie and some dynamics very triggering, yet they wouldn't be so difficult for others to watch. Through our session, we dug into where those feelings came from and what lies I had believed from my own personal experiences. We worked through them, forgave others, figured out what lie I had believed, and asked Jesus what His truth was for me in the situation. I was able to get healing from some of those emotional scars and hear my Father's truth for me.

After the session, I was happy with the progress that we made but voiced my annoyance with the fact that the movie affected me as much as it did. (Having help from a professional was so important for me!) Healing is a hard journey. It'll be harder before it starts to get better. You're tearing that wound open again to properly heal it. My counselor wisely stated not to be annoyed at it, but to look at it like God using an experience to allow me to grow and heal, which is exactly what He did.

This reminded me of one of those foot masks I recently bought, where you soak your feet for an hour wearing these "socks." They say within three to fourteen days, the dead skin on your feet will begin to peel and fall off. Well, let me tell you, it took a good week until I saw anything happen. Then, when it began, it was disgusting. I was embarrassed. I couldn't get the skin to stop peeling off. I tried pumice stones, exfoliating gloves, foot files, and shaving blades to take it all off, but I couldn't keep up with it. It took over a week of focused time and a lot of effort to finally get a handle on it. The end result was that my feet were way softer and healthier; all the dead skin was gone. It was way more work than I had anticipated and a gross process, but the end results were undeniably better than my damaged and cracked heels from before I tried this experiment.

Healing from pain can be similar to that. The result is worth

> *The result of healing from pain is worth it, but the process can be messy!*

it, but the process can be messy! Moving forward, I am trying to have that mindset when things trigger me. Instead of being annoyed by their existence, I will use them as cues and entry points into hurts that need to be healed. How much more helpful does that feel than to be constantly triggered and brought down by old memories and moments that haunt you?

Healthy relationships of any kind take substantial effort. You've got two broken people trying to function in a way that is respectful to each other, all the while not knowing all that person's triggers or past hurts. At times, it can be a little bit like walking through a minefield. I have learned that I care pretty passionately about people. I get attached and I love deeply, making loyalty a strong attribute in my relationships. Loving and feeling deeply is not a bad thing, but it can be a hard thing. I thank God for it because I am able to empathize with others and discern situations. I believe it is a gift from God to help me fulfill my purpose on this earth. It is the same passion and love that sent me on a journey to be a part of over fifty different children's lives in the foster care system, teach hundreds of children in the public school system, and experience beautiful relationships with friends and family throughout my lifetime. Of course, my biggest blessing from living out this God-given trait is the road that led me to adopt my sweet baby girl. I still can't believe I get to be her Mama!

It's also this same passion and love for people that have caused me a lot of heartbreak throughout my lifetime. I remember feeling the sting of rejection as a child in elementary school trying to make friends. I also remember the pain of caring for men romantically too soon or just too far in general, resulting in heartbreak. I remember being in love and engaged, planning an entire wedding, only to have it called off a few months before the date. I felt so blindsided, betrayed, stupid, and utterly heartbroken. I remember the disappointment of feeling unseen and misunderstood by a friend.

The pain that I felt in some of those moments seemed unbearable, and I am so glad that I don't feel the pain anymore. Thankfully, moments with Jesus, along with the passage of time, help heal the wounded heart. This deep-feeling and loving heart of mine has made it hard. What can I say? It's the way God made me, but there are days I wish I didn't feel as much or love as hard.

Throughout the past few years, with increased isolation and tension through COVID-19, pain from relationships seemed to affect me in all aspects of my life. Not just in a romantic relationship or a friendship; it seemed to be a general struggle of pain in dealing with other people. I am quite aware that this all happened during the pandemic and mental health struggles are real. I am assuming others have struggled with these same challenges. Remember how I told you about the winter of 2020; the ski injury, covid, and the break-up? It was much more about just getting through the days than enjoying them. Due to my physical state of struggling to walk after the skiing injury, and being off work, it was so easy to shrink back and keep to myself. Between the two incidents, I was at home, alone, for over two months.

Isolating during sickness made the art of avoiding people easier. It was all a subtle, yet inviting notion. I found the withdrawal happened slowly. I got weary of caring (too much), feeling too needy, and being vulnerable or misunderstood. I also recognized that I was much more easily offended by people. These feelings came from unmet expectations or miscommunication, or just being exhausted from the weight of life; not having the same patience and intent in my relationships.

The emotional distance in my relationships slowly started becoming the reality of some of my friendships. I tried to convince myself that it was just a season and I needed to give myself grace. I believe there was partial truth to that, but now I am aware that Satan used that thought process to keep me isolated. I didn't want to engage in anything that exposed the state of my heart or let someone have the chance to hurt it. I've been there and done that far too many times. I was trying to protect myself from feeling like I wasn't enough.

It's not that I was being a rude or intolerable person. I hope that most often, I still was able to put on that surface level happiness when interacting with people, was able to laugh at jokes, and was still being a kind person. I think it's very easy to isolate ourselves, now, more than ever. Even worse, it's easier to fake that we are okay even when we are not. My close friends could tell something was off, but I wasn't willing to open up about the root of it all.

I had conversations with close friends who felt the same way. We were so tired of being let down by people. I remember friends advising me to just have low, or even, no expectations of people. It seemed a much easier way to live, leaving much less opportunity to be disappointed. It sounded safe to my weary heart at the moment. I clung to that idea and was letting it shape how I lived my life. I was engaging less with friends and thinking that if I spent less time with them, or stopped pursuing their friendship, it would be easier to protect myself and I likely wouldn't experience so much emotional turmoil.

I remember declaring to a friend that I had figured this thing out- low to zero expectations of people was my new mantra in life. In her loving and gracious way, my friend looked at me with some concern. She suggested that a healthier way to look at life would be to love beyond expectation rather than choosing to disconnect completely. At the moment, I agreed sincerely, but it wasn't until after our conversation that I had time to process her suggestion. I love how my friend interacts with people and how she handles relationships. I felt convicted about the way I was living to protect myself; it was not to love others. It was not what Jesus had called me to do. My heart was just so weary that I found myself with little grace for others.

So, that was my challenge. What does it look like to love people beyond expectation? What do you do with those feelings of anger or disappointment when people just mess up? I had to reassess my boundaries with people and also consider the expectations that I had for those in my life. Were they fair? Did I have grace for people? Was I running to friends to fill needs that only my Saviour could fill? Was putting up walls really going to help change those problems or was I creating more issues? I knew something had to change or I was going to find myself more alone, which definitely was affecting my outlook on life. I wasn't feeling excited or confident about my purpose in this season.

Before I go any further, let me state that I am very aware of how complex this issue is. There is a fine line to all of this and I still am figuring it out. It is absolutely essential to have boundaries with people. In some situations, it is necessary and unavoidable to cut ties and create distance. I am not addressing those toxic relationships with this sentiment. I am talking about the day-to-day relationships that are generally life-giving, but have their normal "ups and downs". No human should be placed on a pedestal and be expected to meet our every expectation or need. We are all human and no one can fulfill all those needs for us. Jesus is the only one who can.

When we live as if we need the affirmation of people on a level they can never provide, we are bound to be discouraged. More importantly, we need to find our solace, contentment, and identity in Jesus. He is who we should run to with our needs and expectations. He is our Creator. It is His opinion of us that matters most. Who better to meet our needs than the one who designed us

*Who better to meet our needs than the one who designed us and knows us intricately?*

and knows us intricately? If we learn to run to Him and make Him a priority in our days and lives, we will experience more peace and have more grace for people. That is how we are able to forgive people when they mess up. I know I have made mistakes as a friend too, so I am sure thankful we can all experience forgiveness. We are called to forgive just as Christ forgave us. If I am expecting to be filled by Christ, then I need to make sure I am spending time with Him.

As I look back on that season, I was laying around, feeling sorry for myself, and spending much more time filling my mind with movies and Netflix series than filling my mind with the words of God. This was the majority of my problem. If throughout the day I pursued an unbroken connection with my Creator and asked to see things through His eyes, my interactions with people would likely unfold differently, or at least in my response to them.

I could see that if I didn't make some intentional changes in my life, things would only get worse. So, I began to delete extra apps from my phone that were wasting my time and encouraging me to stay isolated and waste time. I decided to limit my screen time for shows and television. Most importantly, I made plans for how I was going to get plugged back into God's word and made spending time with Him a priority.

As I did that, things started changing. I was reading Acts last week (Acts 2:42-47), and I was learning about how the church was living in this mindset where they were loving each other and providing for each others' needs; the fellowship of believers. They were selling their possessions and land to give the proceeds to those in need. Can you imagine living life that way? I know some people who do and I truly admire them. As I read it, my heart struggled to know what my response would be given the opportunity. Sure, a few dollars here and there, no problem. But selling my home to help other people out? It seemed like a drastic kind of love for another, but inspiring nonetheless. The author of the study I was doing asked us why the church had such unity and asked us to look at John 17:20-26. As I read these words, my eyes filled my tears, knowing that this mindset is what I had been missing all of these months. This is one of the last things Jesus prayed before He was crucified:

> I am not asking on behalf of these alone, but also for those
> who believe in Me through their word, that they may all be
> one; just as You, Father, are in Me and I in You, that they also

*may be in Us, so that the world may believe that You sent Me. The glory which You have given Me I also have given to them, so that they may be one, just as We are one; I in them and You in Me, that they may be perfected in unity, so that the world may know that You sent Me, and You loved them, just as You loved Me. Father, I desire that they also, whom You have given Me, be with Me where I am, so that they may see My glory which You have given Me, for You loved Me before the foundation of the world. Righteous Father, although the world has not known You, yet I have known You; and these have known that You sent Me; and I have made Your name known to them, and will make it known, so that the love with which You loved Me may be in them, and I in them.*

*John 17:20-26, NASB*

It is the most glorious blessing given to the apostles and their relationships with one another- unity! And all to bring glory to God and spread the news of the Gospel. What a wonderful gift to receive! Amongst fellow believers, Jesus declared that they could have the same love and unity that the Father has with the Son. That's mind-blowing to me. It reminded me of how people can support each other and the joy that connection can bring us. It reminded me of what I was missing in my life. Can you imagine if we actually lived like that?

Having friends to do life with is absolutely essential! We need support from others. We need friends to bring us groceries when we are sick and isolated, or to drive us to the hospital when we are single, can't walk or drive, and our families live across the country. We need friends to pray with us and for us, to process events and feelings with us. Friends, and the unity we can have with them when we are believers, is an incredible blessing from the Lord.

I have often read Ecclesiastes 4:9-12 in the context of marriage. However, I think it can be just as easily applied to friendships. This is the kind of friend I want to be, and I am thankful that God has provided me with friends like this:

> Two are better than one, because they have a good reward for their toil. For if they fall, one will lift up his fellow. But woe to him who is alone when he falls and has not another to lift him up! Again, if two lie together, they keep warm, but how can one keep warm alone? And though a man might prevail against one who is alone, two will withstand him—a threefold cord is not quickly broken.
>
> Ecclesiastes 4:9-12, KJV

The third cord in this metaphor is Jesus. When we are in relationship with other believers, that third cord can represent the Holy Spirit in that relationship too.

Life can be difficult; you won't always see eye to eye with people, friends, colleagues, and family. People will likely let you down at some point. It might not even be intentional. People have their own pain and struggles and sometimes can't see past their own situation to notice yours. I was there this year. I blame the brokenness of this world for the hurt that happens between humans. I look forward to a day in heaven when relational turmoil won't be something we have to deal with. For now, be gracious. Find the healthy balance between prioritizing friendships and your pursuit of Jesus in your life. When we prioritize things in the wrong order, it is bound to lead to disappointment.

Our response to anger or bitterness can either be ferocious and boisterous, or it can be passive and withdrawn. Both responses are not how it was intended for us to live with each other. Instead, we are called to peace: "And let the peace of Christ rule in your hearts, to which indeed you were called in one body. And be thankful" (Colossians 3:15, ESV). With the help of the Holy Spirit, we can see Him gently mold our hearts so that we can be more gracious
in our relationships.

Relationships are worth the work! They encourage us and help us along life's adventures and challenges. I am so astounded by the journeys I have walked with friends. The tears we have shed together or the uncontrollable laughter over exhaustion or an inside joke. Mostly, I see how we grow and change through life's experiences. Just as we require the forgiveness of our Father within our relationship with Him, any relationship on earth will require those same dynamics.

All of my close friendships which have thrived because of their authenticity have required candid conversations and humble apologies, followed by forgiveness. We have exchanged words and actions that show the care we hold for our friendship. When each one of those conversations is accomplished in grace and love, it has led to deeper connection and closer relationships down the road.

Forgiveness often fosters freedom and connection within a relationship, but often takes humility to meet each other in that vulnerable place. I pray that in the future, when my heart feels weary, Jesus would graciously remind me of this lesson, so I won't try to walk in my own strength. I encourage you to humble yourself when needed in your relationships so that you can also experience that intimacy that two friends can know when their relationship is rooted in Christ, and they are sensitive to His leading in their interactions with each other.

Who better to meet our needs
than the one who designed us
and knows us intricately?

# An Invitation to Embracing Sustaining Peace

*Peace I leave with you; my peace I give you. I do not give to you as the world gives. Do not let your hearts be troubled and do not be afraid.*

*– John 14:27*

I just want to reiterate that as I write this, the Lord continues to teach me and humble me. There are days when I wake up with the motivation to pursue Jesus and take those moments to connect with Him. When I do that, I can honestly notice the difference in my day; not necessarily with what happens, but in my reaction and perspective. I know that when those days occur, it is clearly because the fruit of the Holy Spirit is flowing through me. Those days are good days. Then there are the days where I fail to connect with Him and choose the more comfortable option of laying down

*Motivation comes and goes; whereas discipline, when fostered correctly, remains when motivation falls by the wayside.*

on the couch to mindlessly numb out to the latest t.v. show recording. Not that tv is bad, but it is rarely doing anything to spiritually encourage my heart or mind. Even though I am tired, I have not nurtured the Holy Spirit's presence, and I can usually see it in my reactions, my parenting, or just my general outlook on life.

I am looking forward to the day when my spiritual maturity and devotion win against my lack of motivation so that I can live daily with the power of the Holy Spirit. I know that I can be a brighter light for Him on those days, and I feel better about myself and my circumstances too, so it's a win-win for everyone.

God uses the most unique things to teach and shape us. At school, I have been doing a novel study with my students. The book we are reading is intended for young children, yet it has been instrumental in reminding me of a pivotal truth, which is the difference between motivation and discipline. Motivation comes and goes; whereas discipline, when fostered correctly, remains when motivation falls by the wayside. We need that in so many aspects of life to thrive. So my personal goal is to have more days when I thrive with spiritual discipline than ones where I slug by with my own comfort and laziness. God is gracious with me in this journey. He will be gracious with you too!

What does peace look like? For me, peace is learning to slow down, and to sometimes even say no to "good things" in order to make room in my life for the most important things. Peace is found in the simplicity of life; heart-to-heart conversations with friends,

> *Peace is the continuation of a humble heart before my Saviour, with gratefulness for where I can see His hand.*

the joy of laughter, and the feeling of being known and enjoying intimate encounters that expand our love of the Father. It looks like a reflection on Jesus' provision for your family. It is the decreasing desire to gain everyone's approval because you walk in the confidence of who God calls you to be. It is knowing that you are HIS and therefore being claimed as someone else's is a secondary aspiration. Peace is the continuation of a humble heart before my Saviour, with gratefulness for where I can see His hand. As a parent, I am seeing that I get less angry. I am seeing Jesus' love in my reactions and parenting more and more with my daughter. It is an improvement and growth, but it certainly isn't because of my own strength. It is Jesus abiding in me.

I still have moments where fear creeps in, anger starts to brew, and insecurity starts to rise up. I can get lost in the unknowns of the future and the feelings of inadequacy. But I find myself more quickly recognizing the drift and returning my gaze back to my heavenly Father, and choosing peace.

It is a daily decision. A moment-by-moment intervening of the Holy Spirit in our thoughts and actions. Because of that, you can go from a worldly way of functioning to a Spirit-led way in the blink of an eye. Connection is key. Corrie ten Boom said it best: *"If you look at the world, you'll be distressed. If you look within, you'll be depressed. If you look at God you'll be at rest."* [17] Return to Him for rest. Set your eyes on Him for peace that will last.

---

17. Mowrer, Kelly. n.d. "Quotes from Corrie Ten Boom." Live at the Well. Accessed November 4, 2022. https://www.liveat-thewell.org/quotes-from-corrie-ten-boom.html.

Peace is the continuation of a humble heart before my Saviour, with gratefulness for where I can see His hand.

_____

# The Abundance of His Sustenance

*I came that they may have life, and have it abundantly.*

*- John 10:10*

It is amazing how God can reinforce the truths that He is teaching me through unexpected avenues. Today at church, our pastor spoke about the wedding at Cana from John 2. He gave us a bit of the historical context for this story. In that time, running out of wine at one's wedding was a public disgrace. The bride and groom simply didn't have enough wine and they were left in this terrible position of failure and disgrace on their wedding day. Through various events, Jesus stepped in. He asked them to trust Him. He called them to fill the jugs with water and to carry them to the priest of the wedding. Miraculously, the water turned to wine, and the bride and groom were congratulated for having the best and most choice wine for the latter part of their wedding celebration. The pastor also explained that the amount of wine that Jesus produced (between 120-180 gallons) would have been worth the equivalent of a year's wage.[18]

My heart erupted with joy as I jumped ahead to the conclusion, recognizing how this ties into what God has been teaching me. He not only met their needs but provided something even richer and better than what they had before. He also provided a ridiculous abundance of wine that would have benefitted them financially as they began the journey of this new season in life as newlyweds. What a blessing! What a gift they would never have received had they run out of wine. Don't you believe that God will do the same for you in your life? I'm

> *He not only met their needs but provided something even richer and better than what they had before.*

sure the bride and groom went through feelings of failure and fear of what this could look like, never imagining the result would have been so much better than what they could have supplied on their own.

As the day passed, my thoughts kept going back to this lesson. I felt God gently encourage me. He asked me to look through the Bible and spend my quiet times with Him on a quest to find as many examples of God blessing people abundantly; not just sustaining them, but giving them an abundance. Often, He asks me to do these things to remind me of what I already know but possibly lost perspective somewhere along the road. This was one of those scenarios.

I initially thought of Moses when God asked him to free the Israelites. Moses was hesitant and felt like he was insufficient. The Lord not only equipped Moses but gave him someone to do the

18. Raymond, Erik. 2018. "Why Did Jesus Make so Much Wine?" The Gospel Coalition. April 18, 2018. https://www.thegospel-coalition.org/blogs/erik-raymond/jesus-make-much-wine/.

speaking for him. Now I know there have been arguments made that Moses should have just trusted God and that he would supply him with what he needed. I love how it shows God's character. Instead of chastising him, He graciously equipped Moses by using another person. I see Him do the same for me throughout life. What a wonderful gift. Not only simply sustaining Moses, but giving him an abundance to thrive and succeed in a task he was destined for.

We've got our classic examples, like Jesus feeding the five thousand from two fish and five loaves of bread, providing an abundance of leftovers. We have the provision of manna for the Israelites, as well as the favour He provided to Esther to be in a place of power to save her people. God even uses His own creation to provide for His people. In Matthew 17, Jesus supplied a coin in the fish's mouth for Peter to pay his temple tax. In 1 Kings 17, God directed the ravens to supply Elijah with food.

I love how He so creatively meets the needs of His people in a multitude of ways. What amazes me is that when you read these accounts in the Bible, they are just stated in a sentence or two like they are a normal occurrence. Yet they are all miracles, but so simply accomplished by our Creator. But isn't that the essence of our God- providing miraculous abundance throughout our lives, in ways we aren't expecting He will? It makes me excited to wait in anticipation for His continued provision in my life.

The Lord not only sustains us in life, He blesses us abundantly in many ways. He also protects us, and I can look back and thank God for not allowing certain things to happen in my life. There are some key moments in life that I can look back on and see God's hand! There are situations that God answered with a no at the time and it broke my heart. For me, there was pain, a lack of understanding, and a genuine loss of hope for the future. Looking back over the decades now, some of those moments where my heart fell apart because God graciously closed a door, I can honestly thank Him for the protection He provided. His grace overwhelms me. It might have been painful at the time, but from where I sit now, intervening was the kindest thing He could have ever done for me.

When I am feeling less than hopeful, I look back and reflect on these times: God leading me through unknown paths that He set my feet upon. He equipped me with what I needed when He sent me, He graciously redeemed me when I felt broken, and He has repeatedly restored me when I failed. He sustained me through the highs and lows of life. I see His grace for me. I see His love for me. He has given me more than I deserve. He has lavished His love upon me.

Life doesn't always pan out how we imagined. That's where faith comes in. It requires trusting Jesus even when it doesn't add up to us. When I think of how Jesus is the architect of my story, it moves me. I feel known. I feel pursued. John Eldredge articulated this idea well when he wrote, *"Every song you love, every memory you cherish, every moment that has moved you to holy tears has been given to you from the One who has been pursuing you from your first breath in order to win your heart."* [19]

God has His own love story for each one of us. It is between you and Him. He longs to bless us with abundant joy. He wants us to experience intimacy with Him and be whole with His joy. This promise of sustenance doesn't mean that we will just get by and barely survive the storms of life. It's way more than that! There is an abundance of love from our Father, an abundance of favour, an

19. Eldredge, John, and Stasi Eldredge. 2005. Captivating : Unveiling the Mystery of a Woman's Soul. Nashville: Thomas Nelson Incorporated.

abundance of peace, an abundance of joy, and an abundance of protection. We just need to have that kingdom perspective and not an earthly one.

> *There is an abundance of love from our Father, an abundance of favour, an abundance of peace, an abundance of joy, and an abundance of protection. We just need to have that kingdom perspective and not an earthly one.*

His abundance is so far beyond our comprehension that He is unfolding things that we couldn't even imagine or had the foresight to ask for. His abundance might be the result of Him shutting a door that we had our sights set on.

I have already shared previously about waiting for my precious daughter; trusting God through the seemingly unanswered prayers that broke my heart. I am so glad that He said no to my other requests so that His better yes could take place. When I look back on all those other sweet children, I pray for their protection and that they also found a loving home. However, I am so ecstatic that God saying no to them meant He had my daughter saved for me. I couldn't have picked a daughter and companion in life more perfect for me if I tried to.

I have also shared about my engagement that ended before we got to the altar; a no that at the time absolutely broke me. Let me tell you how God worked the realities of that situation for my good. After the engagement ended, years passed and I completed two degrees in my efforts to become a teacher. As much as I had moved on, I still carried a burden and sense of rejection from the entire experience. Although I loved my family in Nova Scotia, part of me longed for a fresh start. I want to go to a place where people wouldn't know me from that traumatic time; a place where I had no reminders of the pain and felt no pity. I wanted to go somewhere new.

Consequently, there were also no teaching jobs in Nova Scotia at the time and we were told to expect to be subbing for seven-to-eight years before we'd have a job. These circumstances lead to my heart changing about where I wanted to live, while I established myself during my adulthood.

Amazingly, I got hired at a job fair, eight months before I even finished my Bachelor of Education degree from Acadia University. It was so exciting to be able to finish those eight months with the anticipation of what I would be doing. To be hired ahead of time was not a frequent occurrence; they had given me a contract without a specific position because they said they wanted me as a teacher. For me, it was a welcomed invitation of being noticed and wanted. Even if it was in a professional situation, it still did my heart good. God's timing is so amazing. I think back to that interview and remember they originally told me the district wasn't even going to do interviews. They had come to just make connections. However, there was a snowstorm and they couldn't fly out on their original date. They decided to make the most of the situation and call some of the applicants whom they had received resumes from. They called me and the rest is history.

I had told my parents that if I was offered a job and I felt peace about it, I would say yes and sign the contract, but we all agreed that likely wasn't going to happen as they had given no indication that they were offering contracts. However, my parents and grandparents were all back at home, waiting together to hear the news and praying for wisdom for me in the situation. I remember leaving the hotel conference room with my signed contract in hand, driving through the streets of downtown Halifax bursting with anticipation to tell them the news. When I walked in the door, their eyes met mine with an inquiry as to the result. I announced that I signed a contract and had a job! It was a beautifully complicated moment mixed with conflicting emotions. There were tears of happiness for my success mixed with tears of sorrow with the knowledge that I would be leaving them soon. I am so thankful to have a family that supported me and walked in faith with me even when they knew that the result meant personal loss and pain for them. What a magnificent gift to experience; the unconditional love and support of your loved ones. I still remain thankful.

I had never planned on leaving Nova Scotia, but God had other plans. I moved out west eleven years ago. It required faith and bravery, but I was ready for it! A week after I finished my degree, me, my dad, and my trusted feline Bentley packed up my Hyundai Elantra and drove across Canada to a smaller city in Alberta that I had never even been to before. When I looked at the map of the city I would soon call home, I saw that it had a Costco and knew I'd be fine. Costco only goes to cities where there are larger groups of people, right?

I arrived not knowing a single person. I found an amazing house for rent with a landlord who held it for me for three months because he wanted a good tenant and figured a teacher would be exactly that. God's favour was all over the situation. To top it all off, I got hired to work for the public school district, but within that district was a school of choice which was a Christian school. They had an opening for a new teacher which could turn into a permanent contract, and in my second interview, got hired to work there. So I got to work at a Christian school and get paid a public school teacher wage. Absolutely amazing! The staff were very welcoming as I was the new kid on the block and the youngest by quite a few years. Within a year, I was able to get a permanent contract as well as buy a house. I have felt so blessed by how God has made smooth sailing in this area of my life.

About four years ago, I became a mom and was able to experience the wonderful journey of adoption. A year later, we were able to purchase a home a little bit bigger with a garage for those -45 winters; a master bedroom with a bathroom; and a wonderful kitchen that even has an ice dispenser in the fridge. Now, you may laugh, but as a child, I never thought I would get to a place where I would have my very own ice dispenser attached to my fridge. I remember how excited I was about it!

If I had gotten married at the young age of nineteen, these fifteen years would have been a completely different story. I wouldn't have this career, my wonderful group of friends, or be a mother to my sweet baby girl. I remain single, and I hope that this aspect of my life is yet to be redeemed by Jesus. I work to trust God with it and know that He is capable of bringing a godly man into my life, if, and when He wants. If not, then that's not His best for me right now. Depending on the day, I am sometimes more able to accept that truth than others. He is teaching me day by day to trust in Him and look to Him for joy and contentment.

When I reflect on the financial blessings and security that He has given me, it can make me very emotional. Satan has told me many lies over the years about my singleness. One fear He placed in me was that I wouldn't be able to financially provide for myself on just one income. I had fear about this and remember feeling hopeless about those adult milestones one looks forward to. That has not been the case at all. He has provided me with a beautiful home and honestly, more than I ever dared to imagine. He also provided me with two wonderful parents who also have taught me the value of money and how to manage it well. Without their leadership and advice over my life, I know I would not be in the place where I am. I attribute it all to God. I get overwhelmed at how He has more than sustained me in this area of my life, raining down abundant favour and security.

Sometimes when we think of sustainment, we think of just enough to get by. What I want to point out here is that I can see God's hand of blessing and provision in my life above and beyond what I expected or deserve. I encourage you to reflect on seasons in life and places where God has led you, abundantly blessed you, or just opened those doors wide so that His favour brightly shone down on you. Look back to those moments to strengthen your faith and help you to trust in Him.

As I reminisce over these eleven years since I moved West, I am astounded at the roads He has led me down, the paths and decisions He has protected me from, and the blessings that He had waiting for me on this new and unexpected journey. I have grown professionally and personally. I have met the most amazing people. I honestly feel like I am a different person than the one who moved out here back in her early twenties. Sure, I have made some mistakes along the way and experienced some very painful moments too because of some of my choices. I have also known forgiveness and redemption like I had never experienced before either. There are countless blessings from this season. The best gift has been becoming a mother to my amazing daughter.

I am so thankful for God's redeeming, restoring, and renewing love that has transformed my heart and mind. My life has been marked by His grace and I am excited about the calling He has put on my life to share this news.

> *My son, do not forget my teaching, but keep my commands in your heart, for they will prolong your life many years and bring you peace and prosperity. Let love and faithfulness never leave you; bind them around your neck, write them on the tablet of your heart. Then you will win favor and a good name in the sight of God and man. Trust in the LORD with all your heart and lean not on your own understanding; in all your ways submit to Him, and He will make your paths straight. Do not be wise in your own eyes; fear the LORD and shun evil. This will bring health to your body and nourishment to your bones. Honor the LORD with your wealth, with the first fruits of all your crops; then your barns will be filled to overflowing, and your vats will brim over with new wine.*
>
> *- Proverbs 3:1-10*

What I love about this proverb is the vivid image it provides. We are told where to put our faith and trust and live in an honourable way. Can you honestly put a price on the promise of peace? To have peace in this world is an immeasurable gift. All of these commands have blessings attached to them; each one filled with abundance.

When I was a child, I used to think that God had a lot of rules. I don't know if it was how I interpreted it all or how it was shared with me in certain settings. I always felt like there were just so many rules that I could never be perfect; which in many ways is true. This often left me with a sense of impending failure, mixed with a drive to conduct myself in a way that would be honourable to God. This desire to be perfect seemed to birth out of a mindset of obligation rather than a sense of a loving relationship with my heavenly Father. However, as I have walked through life and have not always made the wisest choices, God has graciously shown me that those rules He put in place, those commands in the Bible, are not there to simply control me or decrease my ability to experience pleasure. They are there to protect me. If I would have followed all of them as He told me, there would have been less pain in my life and the lives of others. Less friction, tension, and turmoil in relationships. Less regret. Less worry. Less fear. Less bitterness. Instead, there would have been more joy. More peace. More security. More connection. More hope. Thankfully, these fruits continue to grow and radiate in my life as I continue to pursue Him.

When I think of God sharing these commands with me now, I hear them in a kind and gentle voice, one that knows of the dangers and wants His cherished child to avoid them. Just like a parent wants to protect their children from the things they know will only cause destruction, God put rules and boundaries in place to protect us from worldly temptations that can also lead us away from Him and into darkness and pain. If you look at the biblical commands that way, instead of a list of dos and don'ts, your entire perspective changes. Your desire to rebel diminishes and your trust in the Father increases. I am sure you can look back on life and see a place where this rings true.

I don't know your story, but what I do know is that it doesn't take long on this earth to experience pain, discomfort, brokenness, and a lack of trust. The road may be long, but you are not walking it alone. The blows may be hard, but you are not left to weather them by yourself. Rest in that truth. Seek after the One who created you, who gives you provision and purpose, and who will allow you to rest in the palm of His hand while He cradles your fall.

Look for opportunities to cultivate hope within your circumstances. My hope board is a culmination of verses, quotes, and notes from beautiful interactions with others who have built me up in Christ. There are objects that hold meaning from life-changing moments that act as reminders that He is for me. It is a reminder that He makes all things beautiful in His time. Our job is to commune with Him in the process and trust Him for the outcome.

While we wait, we are called to enjoy the journey and live in a way that can build others up in their faith. When I look at my hope board, it is an instant reminder, to my heart, of the love of my Saviour. I cannot deny His provision and purpose in light of how He speaks to me, affirming me of His unconditional love. My hope board is a continual source of renewal and revelation. I encourage you to create some sort of hope board for yourself, that could be a source of motivation for your heart; personalized to your unique walk with your Saviour. It is a powerful and practical tool that aids in keeping hope in the forefront of your mind.

When I remain in Him, I feel secure. I know, beyond a shadow of a doubt, that He is my Sustainer. I walk with a certain confidence. He is the one who can wipe away the slow, numbing pain of this

*Not only does He provide for you, but He pursues you. He is deeply in love with you and delights in giving you good things. He has good plans for your life!*

world that functions in brokenness. This brokenness presents itself in fear, anger, bitterness, feelings of insufficiency, feeling justified to grumble, a fixation on unmet longings, and loneliness. He can remove and negate these broken ways of functioning and replace them with unshakeable peace, unwavering faith, a renewed sense of hope, an awareness of our abundant blessings, an attitude of grace, gratitude, and contentment, and an exuberant confidence in our sense of worth and security in Him. Not only will He sustain you with His provision, but He will bless you abundantly.

Not only does He provide for you, but He pursues you. He is deeply in love with you and delights in giving you good things. He has good plans for your life! This is a truth that I have started declaring over my daughter and me during our bedtime prayers. I want us to live with the revelation that God is for us. He created us in His image and He knows our worth. He is the source of our worth.

Remember that He holds you up. He guides you. He gives you the nourishment you need and provides for you through those whom He brings into your life. Be blessed, my dear friend. Find solace under His wings. Keep your mind and heart expectant on the blessings of His sweet sustenance.

Not only does He provide for
you, but He pursues you.

# Epilogue

Writing this book has been a journey and a gift. It has been a reflective time for me to look over my life with a lens of finding His sustenance, followed by His abundant blessings. I have only been surprised and encouraged to see things from the viewpoint of His sustenance. It has made my hope greater, my faith stronger, and my desire to remain in an unbroken connection with the Saviour all the more desirable. I thank you for following me on this journey. I sincerely hope that you have been blessed and encouraged by my stories and reflections. I hope that it has given you a fresh perspective on some of your circumstances as well as an energized vision for your future. One that you can trust God has good plans for. He can take the scars and pain of your life and use them for your good and the good of those who are brought into your path! I know He has done this in my life and will continue to in the future.

I end with a reflection from my last birthday, simply to exemplify that we all go through seasons. You may be at peace in one week and then have something happen the next that causes you to reset your perspective and cling to Jesus. As humans, we are not immune to the woes of the world, to being weighed down by the pressures and feelings of inadequacy. When those times come, don't feel as though you are a failure because you are struggling internally. Run back to Him. Be honest with Him! He loves you and wants to hear from you regardless of your state.

Today was my thirty-fourth birthday. I find birthdays can be a hard thing because as humans, we use them as a time to gauge our life's success and see if we are on track with our timeline; that's right, OUR timeline. I tend to be mostly satisfied with my current situation in life. I have moments of longing but overall, I am content and happy being single. However, when my birthday comes around, it is a real struggle. That's when the little voice in my head tells me I am getting older and still alone... That there is something wrong with me to still be alone at this age. I think this year, spiritual warfare was happening (possibly because I am writing this book) and it was even harder. I woke up with sadness and felt embarrassed by it because I know I have so much to be thankful for, but I just felt lonely and like I was failing at life because I was alone.... I explained these thoughts to God as I opened my bible and sat on my bed with tears rolling down my cheeks. I opened up to the passage in John where Jesus is talking about the parable of the shepherd and the sheep, and us knowing His voice. But the part that stuck out to me was, *"I came that they may have life, and have it abundantly"* (John 10:10, ESV)! That is what I was wanting-abundant life; joy-filled life, because of the Spirit! My eyes were drawn to the part right before where he warns us that the thief has come to steal, kill and destroy... Satan; that's his game. I knew the lies I was believing about my worth and my loneliness were total lies that were set out to destroy me and bring me down. So with all the determination I was able to muster, I prayed that I would live today seeing myself how God sees me and feeling loved because of His love for me- to renounce the lies. I am not alone. God is with me, and He has blessed me with amazing friends who surround me, support me, and celebrate me, especially today.

I told Him it felt disrespectful to be so sad when I have so much. I asked Him for joy and perspective; to have grace-filled expectations of people and just enjoy my life... my daughter, my class, and the friends who I was going to have dinner with that night.

The day passed and with it were sweet moments of surprise from a surprise birthday lunch that my students planned for me, to phone calls with loved ones, ending the day with dinner at Montana's with my closest friends. My beautiful friend who had planned my birthday party paid for supper and was even purchasing a Wonder Woman-themed dairy queen cake to celebrate me. This overwhelmed me with her generosity and it touched my heart. I felt so loved and so cared for.

As I processed my thoughts about the day, I was reminded that I am the furthest thing from alone. Yes, it's true that I don't have a romantic partner to waltz throughout life with, but I have my Saviour, a wonderful family, and an absolutely fantastic group of friends who step in to fill so many gaps that a traditional family dynamic would provide. I started the day with angst and despair, called out to Jesus, and watched Him work through my heart and mind throughout the day.

As I sit here tonight, I am in a different headspace and feeling overwhelmingly blessed by my friends. All of my closest friends are believers as well and I can honestly say that the same Holy Spirit living in me was evident in them today, to reach out to me and shower me with love on my birthday.

Oh, how His grace sustains me, how His provision is abundant and surprising. Every prayer is answered- sometimes with a yes, sometimes with a no, and sometimes with the word wait. Resting in His power and His ultimate good plans for our lives renews our spirit in a world that attacks hope. Find it in Him. Living with hope and expectation of how He will meet my needs provides a certain adventurous appeal. It's not all about me, but Him. In His goodness, He delights in blessing me. He loves me. The creator of the universe wants to meet my needs and my desires when they are in alignment with His truth. I get lost in the complexity of this truth. But I keep my eyes open, waiting with anticipation to be humbled by how He is so good to me. My prayer is that if this is not already a personal revelation for you, it will be soon. To shift to this perspective makes each day and interaction one that exudes more of His grace and sustenance. I end with this blessing from 2 Corinthians 13:14,

> *Every prayer is answered- sometimes with a yes, sometimes with a no, and sometimes with the word wait. Resting in His power and His ultimate good plans for our lives renews our spirit in a world that attacks hope.*

*"May the grace of the Lord Jesus Christ, and the love of God, and the fellowship of the Holy Spirit be with you all."*

# About the Author:

A born and raised Maritimer, Julianna Davidson currently resides in Grande Prairie, Alberta with her spunky and joy-filled daughter. She is an Elementary School teacher who has a passion for writing and a heart for those hurting, with the desire to renew hope in the midst of their circumstances. She leads worship at her local church, enjoys experimenting with potential culinary masterpieces, songwriting by the fire on a cold, wintry night, perusing thrift stores for unexpected literary finds,paddle boarding at sunset and packing up the trailer and hitting the road for the latest camping adventures with her friends, family and loyal pups.